YOUNG WRITERS

ALL ABOARD FOR

BERKSHIRE

First published in Great Britain in 1995 by
POETRY NOW
1-2 Wainman Road, Woodston,
Peterborough, PE2 7BU

All Rights Reserved

Copyright Contributors 1995

SB ISBN 1 85731 584 7

Foreword

Toot, Toot! All Aboard! Set sail on a fantastic journey through the minds of today's children. Along the way we hope you will be charmed and enlightened by the thoughts, feelings and humour expressed by these young writers.

The poems included in this anthology have been selected for their exciting imagination, depth of feelings and down to earth language; revealing these children's awareness of various important issues close to many of our hearts. Now you can finally find out what these children *really* think of their parents, teachers and why trees lose their leaves in autumn!

We hope that you will sit back and enjoy this on-board entertainment, and we wish you a pleasant journey. Bon voyage!

CONTENTS

Aldermaston CE School

	Elaine Shirt	1
	Lynette Chilver	1
	Laura Coventry	2
	Thomas Bailey	2
	Titus Wardle	3
	Colin Day	4
	Claire Methven	4
	Natalie Thomas	5
	Kim Pinkard	6
	Eleanor Hunt	7
	Laura Thomas	7
	Lyndsay Broadhurst	8
	Kate Munro-Ashman	8
	Chloe Macdonald	9
	Felix Wardle	9
	Sebastian Thomas	10
	Lucy Bailey	10
	Zara Rumble	11
	Rebecca Stedham	11
	Esther Wilkins	12
	Selina Barlet	13
	Natalie Bartlett	14
	Rachel Tucker	14

Beechwood Primary School

	Frazer Bright	15
	Laura Thumwood	16
	Clare Curtis	16
	Raymond Bush	17
	Lisa Walker	17
	Penny New	18
	Dwayne Winter	18
	Louise Cox	19
	Vernon Lee	19
	Laura Rushton	20
	Jane Squires	20
	Samantha Mancey	21

Louise Proctor	21
Louise Pegg	22
Rachel Bowker	22
Christopher Rich	23
Michael Williams	23
Hayley Cowcher	24
Tom Hartnell	24
Nikki Macedo	25
Neil Warlow	25
Nick Birch	26
Sarah Squires	26
Rhiannon Phillips	27
Kim O'Reilly	28
Laura Serafin	28
Vikki Aust	29
Cathy Stoter	30
James Reynolds	30
Claire Gowler	31
Katie Bell	31
Robert Dean	32
Jonathan Norton-Standen	33
Melanie-Jayne Radburn	33
Victoria Crombie	34
Francesca Carrisi	34
Michael Halpin	35
Matthew Walsha	35
Peter Brown	36
Chris Jones	36
Lee Cowcher	37
Chris Blackall	37
Claire Carter	38

Brightwalton CE Primary School

Kerri Mack	38
Michelle Drennan	39
Charlotte Clarke	39
Emily Clarke	40
Lottie Beaumont	40

Caversham Primary School

Anna Wise — 41

Crazies Hill CE School

Lucy Claire Hounsom — 42
Victoria Cope — 43
Tammie Hiscock — 43
Kelley Hiscock — 44
Zoe Brooker — 44
Joanne Hendry — 45
Louisa Sidery — 45

Courthouse Junior School

Ian E S Higgins — 46
Amy Lyczba — 46
Kiran Sinhal — 47
Julie-Ann Allen — 47
Emma Hill — 48
Joel Stacey — 48
Leah Bowers — 49
Andrew Collins — 49
Sarah Haunton — 50
Hannah Hunt — 50
Rachel Garland — 51
Louise McCarthy — 51
Michelle Henry — 52
Jenny Mathieson — 52
Louise Jell — 53
Emily Noden — 53
Gary Jacklin & Luke Baxter — 54
Tom Wallis — 54
Samantha Richards — 55
Hamish Harris — 56
Charlotte Rumble — 56
Christiane Jell — 57
Lara Easton — 58
Rosie Heath — 58
Gemma Taylor — 59
Layla Stevenson — 59
Jonathan Stuart — 60

	Richard Price	60
	James Hawkes	61
Churchend Primary School		
	Sarah Jennings	61
	Shoshana Ross	62
	Carly Burke	63
	Danielle Cserfalvi	63
Crown Wood School		
	Sarah Wanklyn	64
	Natalie Wright	64
	Samantha Brown	65
	David Bird	65
	Jessica Ballytine	66
	Heather Fernley	66
	Rachel Wilkinson	67
	Christina Butchers	67
	Wendy Brown	68
	Hollie Brightman	68
	Lee Avery	69
	Amy Gillard	70
	Terri Lochyer	71
	Charlene Corrigan	71
Claycots Middle School		
	Hannah Chapman	72
	Anthony Proctor	72
	Victor Charles	73
	Sheetal Sharma	73
Fox Hill School		
	Alison Corney	74
	Vicky Novelle	74
	Maria Filby	75
Great Hollands Junior School		
	Laura Fallon	75
	Hannah Findlay	76
	Matthew Bettison	76
	Lindsay Nash	77
	Heidi Clay	77
	Aimee Dale	78

	Jamie Hobden	78
	Joel Baker	79
	Christopher Tarry	80
Harmans Water Junior School		
	Daniel Brown	81
	Jenny Grace	82
	Elizabeth Clark	82
	Matthew Burnett	83
Hungerford CP School		
	Charlotte Thatcher	83
	Josh Finesilver	84
	Laura Horne	84
	Emma Hunter	85
Lynch Hill Combined School		
	Rebecca Moore	86
	Lisa Fraser	86
	Anthony Mathews	87
	Damien Woodall	88
	Joanna Hussey	89
	Hayley Lightfoot	90
Nine Mile Ride CP School		
	John Briggs	91
Our Lady of Peace Middle School		
	Toni D'Amaro	92
	Peter Donnelly	92
	Christopher Loudon	93
	Kirsty Akehurst	94
	Roshni Vadher	94
	Lorraine McGuckian	95
	Aaron Bond	95
	Denise Morris	96
	Raymond Stahacz	97
	Rebecca Sheldon	97
	Justin Munt	98
	Angela Mullix	99
	Anna Noctor	100
	Natasha Reddy	100
	Joelle Dupont	101

Natasha Ansari	102
Tony O'Donnell	102
Amanda Button	103
Katie-Sian Power	104
Daniel Almeida	104
Emma-Louise Walton	105
Elizabeth Jane Kennedy	106
Siobhan Taylor	106
Kevin Loughlin	107
Hayley Peters	107
Paual Kerins	108
Tarandip Rehal	109
Nick Bell	109
Sean Ryan	110
Nathan Wood	110
Emma Shearer	111
Michael James	112
Lauren Godfrey	112
Sebastien Butcher	113
Niall Brophy	114
Gina Mundee	114
Claire Griffin	115
Erin Brown	116
Fiona Green	116
Richard Swiatek	117
James Cook	118
Georgia Mann	118
Jenna Graham	119
Sarah O'Shea	120
Richard Wheeler	120
Chris Arthur	121
Vibha Vadher	121
James Carpenter	122
Clare McLaughlin	122
Bharan Kumar	123
Michael McCormack	123
Rhia Daniell	124
Ashley James	124

	Becky Campion	124
	Chloé Thornton	125
	Bina Thakrar	125
	Hannah Webb	126
	Luke Davies	126
	Louise O'Reily	127
	Andrew Seymour	127
	John Millican	127
	Michelle Cox	128
Parsons Down Junior School		
	Charlotte Henderson	128
	Michelle Mason	129
	Luke Dixon	130
	Scott Newport	131
	Catherine Holland	132
	Nikki Arnold	132
	Karen Swanborough	133
	David Caswell	134
	Neil Edlin	135
	Jaimie Davies	136
	Dominic Howard	137
	Melissa Banbury	138
	Sam Bishop	139
	Shauna Saunders	140
Ranikhet Primary School		
	Jennifer Bristow	140
	Kristina Bray	141
	Hayley Walker	141
	Kirsty Bradfield	142
	Kailey Bennellick	142
	Luke Grover	143
	Kylé Holland	143
Sandy Lane Junior School		
	Natalie Jackson	144
	Stuart Graham	144
	Philip James Munday	145
	Michael Sheldon	145
	Rhea Carter	145

Adam Lippett	146
Neil McAlees	146
Sian Dempsey	146
Chris Anderson	147
Rosemary Modi	147
Sarah De Caux	148
David Garstang	148
Hollie Roach	148
Laura Bryant	149
Bryn Chainey	150
Bianka Roberts	150
Mark Wilson	151
Gillian Underdown	151
Robin Lindsay-Kipp	152
Rachel Muttock	152
Siobhan Stapleton	153
Lee Nicholls	153
Kerri Evanson	154
Laura Keeble	154
Mark Newell	154
Tanya Swain	155
Katy Hanbury	155
Sean Cahill	156
Rachel Ward	156
Twyla Melanie Holland	157
Joe Keefe	157
Sarah Symes	158
Lianne Osborn	158
Emma Blackall	159
Ben Pocock	159
Kyle Taylor	160
Adam Minns	160
Jemma Parsons	161
Sam Wortley	162
Michael Drury	162
Sean Knight	163
Joseph Winters	163
Frank Neville	164

	Rachel Martin	164
	Stephen Pilkington	165
	Andrew Rouse	165
	Darren Tibby	166
	Enrica Stevens	166
	Michael Reading	167
	Mark Evans	168
	Marcia Peterson	168
	Ruth Brooks	169
	Ashleigh Handley	169
	Laura Wortley	170
	Rebecca Durbin	170
	John Knight	171
	Terry Devine	171
	Elisa Coleman	172
	Harry Levey	172
	Jenni Day	173
	Alex Pobgee	173
	Frances Carr & Hannah Morris	174
	Charlotte Gaskin	175
	Alex Keefe	176
Shaw-Cum-Donnington School		
	Zhala Jordan	176
St Mary's School, Mortimer		
	Joanna Rhoderick	177
	Inneka Evans	177
	Hannah St Paul	178
	Charlotte Haines	178
	Rupert Hetherington	179
	Rosie Wilkin	179
	Rachel Overett	180
	Melanie Hillyard	180
	Philippa Bell	181
St Mary's CE Junior School, Thatcham		
	Jolene Taylor	182
	Emily Barker	182
	Emily Clarke	183
	Rachel Manser	184

St Mary's Primary School, Winkfield

Lindsey Edwards	184
Cara Hawkes	185
Claire Hipkin	186
Timothy Zacks	186
Clare Fisher	187
Samantha Whitfield	187
Andrew Park	188
Clare Coughlan	188
Sarah Badham-Thornhill	189
Bethan Denman	189
Jessica Williams	190
David Kayser	190
Laura Jane Bartlett	191
Kirsten Jardine	191
Jamie Barber	192
Ryan Jones	192
Hayley Bolland	193
Clare Powell	193
Tom Powell	194
Jack Tickner	194
Lloyd Matthews	195
Helen Morton	195
Jennifer Hills	196
Louise Ingham	196
Naomi Kasaska	197
Cassie Cella	197
Stuart Bennett	198
Ryan Godding	198
Edward Cooper	198
Nicholas Chapman	199
Francesca Heath	199
Talli Haim	200
Sarah Colborn	200
Sarah Nagalewska	201
Emily Murphy	201
Laura Finnieston	202
Laura Cronk	202

	Amy Grainger	203
Waltham St Lawrence School		
	Peter Jones	204
	Robert Taylor	204
Whiteknights CP School		
	Helen Vincent	205
	Julia Pike	206
	Andrew Walter	206
	Aimee Driscoll	207
	Victoria Joslin	208
	Thomas Green	208
	David Morgan	209
	Heather Gibson	210
	Michael Mikhail	210
	Jessica Pritchard	211
	Christpher Longhorn	212
Wildridings Primary School		
	Catherine Young	212
	Vikki Docherty	213
	Felicity Morris	213
	Danielle Estcourt	214
	Alice Ludlow	214
	Christpher Hotson	215
	James Waring	215
	Laura Osman	216
	Claire May	216
	Carl Tingley	217
	Robert Phelan	217
	Robert Escott	218
	Matthew East	218
	Chloe Everall	219
Woodley CE Primary School		
	Claire Eastment	219
	Ian Gardener	220
	Carla Morley	220
	Laura Home	221
	Lindsay Clare Muscroft	221
	Jillian Rankin	222

	Mark Saunders	222
	David Ian Riley	223
	Laura Viles	223
	Jenna Smith	224
	Emily Aylward	224
	Sarah Abraham	225
	Charlie-Jane Bryant	225
	Rebecca Bennett	226
	Sam Cialis	226
	Michelle Bennett	227
	Anthony Thompson	228
	Laura Tysoe	228
	Katherine Williams	229
	Becky Viles	229
	Rosanne Warner	230
	Kelly Warwick	230
	Scott Weal	231
	Stephen Parker	231
	Richard Tollman	232
	Thomas Goodey	232
	Charlotte Evans	23
Yattendon School		
	George Hood	233
	Thomas Wills	234
	Faye Bethan Smith	234
	Lesley King	235
	Laura Collett	235
	Lindsey Wakefield	236
	Hannah Keogh	236
	James Ash	237
	George Wood	237

MY TERRIBLE SISTER

My terrible sister is a pain,
She's always doing things wrong,
We went to see my auntie Jane,
But she gobbled her up in one,

We went to London to see the Queen,
But my sister moaned for a Coke,
While we were out the Queen appeared,
And my sister killed her for a joke,

My sister may be a murderer,
But I love her all the same,
And you'll never guess what happened,
When my great aunt Edna came!

Elaine Shirt (10) Aldermaston CE School

TEDDIES

Teddies Teddies big
and small,
Thin ones fat ones scruffy and tall,

Teddy bears Teddy bears all around,
Teddy bears Teddy bears tanned or
browned,
Sitting on the sunny beach,
Look Tubby's eating a peach,
Bungle, Fred, Jimmy and Joe,
They've gone swimming oh don't forget
Moe.

Teddies Teddies big and small,
Thin ones fat ones scruffy
and tall.

Lynette Chilver (11) Aldermaston CE School

DROP DEAD FRED!

The fields were stained with it - bodies and blood,
It ran thick in a mixture amongst the mud.
The remains of people, arms, hands and legs,
This is the work of drop *dead* Fred.

A cutlass in his only arm, a bird balanced on his shoulder;
He paused - ready to pounce, from behind a huge great boulder.
His target stood there unaware of the dangers that stood before him.
Then with a huge great big leap, his culprit lost a limb.

Weak and helpless he lies,
Another victim dies.
All brawn and no brain, drop dead Fred
All of his partners in fighting, *dead!*

Laura Coventry (10) Aldermaston CE School

HAUNTED ISLAND

On the horizon of an endless sea,
The mist never lifts,
It's rather scary,
The overgrown grass covers the gravestones,
You can hear the wind whistling about,
Through the chapel in and out,
The church bells begin to ring,
A choir of ghosts begin to sing,
A black stalker creeps through the bushes,
Whilst a witch on a broom away she rushes.

Thomas Bailey (11) Aldermaston CE School

CARP

Out flies my line,
The weight's like a bomb,
As it forces line to peel off my spool,
It's going to the mark in the middle of the pool,
Now comes the wait,
Oh!
Here we go,
A jerk on the rod,
As a fish makes a run,
I strike,
Now I'm in,
This is a big one,
I have to get it in,
It darts all around,
It's stealing my line,
Crikey it's strong,
I bet you it's big,
Yes!
It's tiring now,
But still taking line,
I slip in the net,
As I steer the fish over the mesh,
I lift up the net,
Wow!
It's big,
Now it's in the weigh sling,
It's a 35 pounder,
My biggest carp ever!
I slip it back,
And it shoots off to sulk.

Titus Wardle (10) Aldermaston CE School

THE GUNK MONSTER

The gunk monster is,
a great ball of gunk.
I got up too close,
and it really really stunk.

It smelt of old jelly,
and old rotten cake,
I took a deep breath,
'Cos I felt rather faint.

It hides out in your bedroom,
then jumps upon your head,
Next minute you know it,
you're feeling rather dead.

The gunk monster is dangerous,
so take lots of care,
its stench is rather deadly,
beware, beware, beware.

Colin Day (10) Aldermaston CE School

BLOSSOM

Blossom blossom on the ground,
Blossom blossom all around.
Blossom blossom on the trees,
Blossom blossom for the bees.

Claire Methven (8) Aldermaston CE School

THE MONSTER DOWN SMELLY ALLEY

There he sits
Day and night
Gobbling food
Out of sight.

Saturday night
What is next?
Pork chops fried
Then custard pies
Then maybe
A can of Coke
He coughs then
He chokes.

If you ever
Go down there
Beware, beware
The monster of
Smelly Alley
Is there!

So if you don't
Want to be eaten
Take the warning
Bring him food
Or be beaten!

Natalie Thomas (11) Aldermaston CE School

THE LAST TIGER

Shush there he is,
The last of the tigers,
Tall, noble and proud,
Why do we persecute them?

Shush there he is,
The last of the tigers,
A beautiful beast,
So tall!
With a reddy-brown smile,
I think he's beautiful,
(that's all).

I know people need to eat,
Ones who are skinny and thin,
And I guess a tiger,
Makes a very good meal,
Meat and a nice tiger skin, skin.

But if we're not careful,
They will become extinct,
The beautiful creature
With black stripes,
With a swishy long tail,
And a fearful *roar,*
Please don't kill them
any more!

Shush there he is,
The last of the tigers,
Tall, noble and proud,
Why do we persecute them!

It's now or never!

Kim Pinkard (11) Aldermaston CE School

DOWN BY THE LAKE SIDE

The geese call,
As a flutter of feathers go into the sky,
As dusk falls,
The geese fall silent in the darkness,
All is dead but not quite,

The wind whistles,
Like a gentle sigh,
While the children play, laugh,
And cry.

As the children leave,
They laugh no more,
Everything is silent,
Except what I saw.

Eleanor Hunt (10) Aldermaston CE School

VE DAY

The flags are flying madly.
The buses are getting stuck,
The dustbin lids are coming off
The flash of rockets have struck.

You could hear the shouting everywhere
The screaming counts as well,
You can hear the people singing,
They're really happy you can tell.

You are very happy sometimes,
but then you think of the dead,
The feeling that's inside you,
stays inside your head

Laura Thomas (9) Aldermaston CE School

AUNTIE MABLE

Knock knock
A knock at the door
The knock I dread
The sort of knock that makes you want to be dead
A shout from the stairs
'Open the door it's auntie Mable'
I shouted back
'I can't I'm hiding under the table'
Then auntie Mable stepped inside
Now I thought, I really have to hide
Then she said 'Come out from the table
It's only me your auntie Mable.'
'Come here, let me give you a kiss'
Oh what a whopper I can't put up with this.
I ran out the door, shouted 'Mum I'm calling for Kate'
Mum shouted back 'OK love don't be late'
And then finally I ran away and didn't come back till the next day.
Then my auntie returned to Yorkshire where the other nightmare aunties joined her.

Lyndsay Broadhurst (11) Aldermaston CE School

UNDERWATER TREASURE

The water splashed by my ears,
I swam to the surfers,
I touched something strange like a
sultana,

A fender and chain,
A lump of amber,
A needle of bone,
And a brooch of bronze.

Kate Munro-Ashman (9) Aldermaston CE School

THE RSPCA

Animal cruelty,
Should be banned.
You try running
From a cruel and wicked
Hand.

Poor young puppies,
Abandoned day and night.
The poor little things
Get such a big fright.

The cats and kittens,
Are taken in and left.
And they're hardly ever
Taken back to the vets.

Remember we're for *life*
        not just for
                Christmas

Chloe Macdonald (10) Aldermaston CE School

VICTORY!

The clanging on the dustbins
and the thumping on the doors.
The banging of the rockets and
the laughing of the crowds.
The crackling of fire with banners
flying high.
The stamping of feet mixed with the
beeping of the buses.
      O Victory
               in Europe!

Felix Wardle (8) Aldermaston CE School

TOM THE TORNADO

I'm rough I'm tough
I'm ripping houses up
I'm strong I'm bold
I'm taking old trees down
I'm big I'm tall
I was never very small
I knock down houses
I up root trees
      that's me Tom
      the tornado.

Sebastian Thomas (8) Aldermaston CE School

WINTER ROBIN

Now is the time when Robins call,
His head is white with snow.
Winter berries grow on the bushes,
And so the rivers flow.

On chilly winter nights,
Robins sleep up in nests,
At great heights.

Through the quiet hours of night,
Happily chirp in their flight.
Is the Robin full of delight.

Lucy Bailey (9) Aldermaston CE School

SPRING

Above the swelling stream,
the air is sweet,
and through the quiet hours,
the little hares meet.

It's in autumn and spring,
that the north wind is blowing,
and in summer's bright dawn,
the new light is coming.

The most magnificent of sights,
The fretful horse stamps at night,
when robin calls it wakes up all,
under the hedges of Gaul

Zara Rumble (9) Aldermaston CE School

A SUMMERY SEASON

A summery sun in summer,
Where the days are long and light
Or a wintry day in winter
Where it's all squashed up and tight

When it's long and light in summer
The birds are singing a song
Blackbirds are feeding their baby birds,
And the trees are growing long

The wind's blowing breezily,
Through the gushing trees
The snow dropping slowly on the mushy leaves

Rebecca Stedham (9) Aldermaston CE School

THE GHOST GIRL

The mist surrounds the gloomy churchyard
In the dead of night.
None can hear her silent footsteps
As she glows so white.
Not a human on earth can see her
As she walks towards the gate
Not except for I that is
In the pale night's light.
For I can see her white dress flowing
In the freezing wind
And I can see her sad cold face
For I'm her only friend.

The ghost girl walks on down
the path
And opens the rotting wood gate
The full moon shines brightly down
on her
In these hours so late.
The clock strikes one
And she turns back
And walks up the gloomy path.
The graveyard was still as still can be
as she stood and looked in fear
She took a glance and out of air
She began to disappear.

Esther Wilkins (10) Aldermaston CE School

THE ONLY CHEETAH

Creeping over the dry, grassy plain,
The only cheetah's hunting ground.
Powerful shoulders and sharp claws,
He stalks, and pounces,
Fails.

Bounding over the sandy ground,
The only safe resting place -
A rocky cliff.
His ribs show clearly through his bedraggled fur,
A picture of hunger.

Lying exhausted in the scorching sun,
No-one to lie down beside him.
Panting breathlessly,
His energy melting away from him.
Weak.

A sharp turn of his head,
He runs away.
Fast, faster, not fast enough.
The sound of a shotgun echoes across the plain.
The only cheetah - gone.

Selina Barlet (11) Aldermaston CE School

THE LITTLE SCRUFFY BOY

There's a little boy down our road he
keeps picking his nose. He's got scabs and
cuts all over because he keeps falling
over. He's always eating sweets and candy,
lolly pops and shandy he doesn't listen to
his mum and he always sucks his thumb.

He gets old worms that slither along
and picks them up with his mum's new tongs.
And chases a little girl called Harriet who
wished she had a chariot. Drawn with white
groomed horses with wispy tails, while she
sits in the back with a bag of snails.

Natalie Bartlett (11) Aldermaston CE School

KING HENRY THE 8TH

King Henry the 8th
What a chap
Gems on his clothes
Gems on his hat.

He had six wives
The 1st one divorced.
The 2nd one beheaded
The 3rd one died
Oh what will Henry decide
I'll have another 3 wives
The same happened to them
But the sixth survived

He had 3 children
Edward, Mary and Elizabeth
Edward died when he was 12
A few years later Elizabeth became
Queen but that's another story

Rachel Tucker (9) Aldermaston CE School

BUBBLES

Floating softly through the air,
Not yet ready to pop.
The pale white bubble flying low,
Past the village square.
Over hills, meadows so green,
Until it popped.
      So I blew another bubble.

Past the oak tree,
With leaves so musty.
Past my house,
With a shimmering shine.
I hoped it could be mine,
Until it popped.
      So I blew another bubble.

There it goes,
High and low.
Past my school,
Over our swimming pool.
Past a parked car and over our road.
Up into the sky,
Very high, goodbye.

Frazer Bright (10) Beechwood Primary School

MONSTERS

There was a monster chasing me,
His nose was black and dusty,
His skin was brown and rusty.

There was a monster chasing me,
I hid right under the bed,
Just as he was turning a
very pale red.

There was a monster chasing me,
It gobbled me to the bone.
But when my mum heard about
it, she didn't even groan.

Laura Thumwood (10) Beechwood Primary School

MOTEL

The Prince Hotel is a stately place to stay
Swimming pools, darts and dominoes to occupy
your day.
In the leaflet it displays the prim and proper ways
to enjoy the highlife holiday.
When you get to the Prince's door,
You are greeted by manure,
And when you get inside there is no floor.
Explorers come to see,
A ginormous spider spree,
Spinning and grinning in room 3.
If the German in room 9 thinks your
clothes are clean and fine,
He'll be selling them at market in no time!
I've been there for a stay,
So you just push away,
Those pretty thoughts of highlife holiday.

Clare Curtis (11) Beechwood Primary School

ANGER

Anger is a really heated ball of fire.
It tastes like burning hot curry.
It smells like burnt ashes from a burning hot fire.
It looks like the planets are all red and
another war.
It sounds like double bass drums going
all over the place.
It feels like overwhelming floods going
over you.

Raymond Bush (11) Beechwood Primary School

MAGICAL DREAMS

As yonder sun creeps slowly to its earthly bed,
And the shining ones come out to chase.
My head filled with day's wrong doings,
Rests soundly on my slumber case.
Those troubled thoughts of greed and darkness,
Those worrying deeds of guilt and dread.
All cease for now my dreams advance,
Smothering all black magic as I rest my weary head.

Lisa Walker (11) Beechwood Primary School

ANGER

Anger is started by something
burning inside.
Anger smells like dead flowers.
Anger looks horrible, like
pollution and death.
Anger tastes like my mum's hot
Chilly.
Anger sounds like rage and
shouting!
But worst of all, it's like the earth
burning and dying.

Penny New (9) Beechwood Primary School

WRIGHTY AND TEAM MATES

Mersons Mersons
on the ball
passes to
Ian Wright
What a shot
What a goal
from
Ian Wright

Seaman with a wicked save
wacks it to Mersons
Mersons passes to Hartson
and Hartson to Ian Wright
Wow wow wow
What a
goal again

Dwayne Winter (11) Beechwood Primary School

POLLUTION

The world is such a lovely place,
Full of wondrous joy.
But the only thing that we do,
Is treat it like a toy.

The world gives us happiness,
The world gives us pleasure.
The world is a precious thing.
A thing that we should treasure.

The flowers are slowly going,
Making way for new roads,
As the concrete's being mixed,
Making up new loads.

Some toys you can fix,
Some toys you can bend.
But this toy I assure you,
You won't be able to mend.

Louise Cox (10) Beechwood Primary School

INSECTS NO!

Insects are nasty. Some crawl, some fly;
I would be happy if they would die.
One night I tried to kill as many as I could
But they all ran under this big chunk of wood.
After this happened I went back to bed
Then a big spider jumped on my head.
This made me mad, not to mention sad,
So I didn't bother with insects any more;
I just let them crawl all over the floor.
I like insects now.
I don't seem to like dogs though:
They all stink like hell!

Vernon Lee (10) Beechwood Primary School

DRUGS

I thought my friend was really cool,
but now she is such a silly fool
When I found out she was taking drugs,
she then told me she only goes to pubs.
She hangs around with dirty men,
what a coincidence they're all called Ben.
But that's not the point,
she likes smoking a joint.
I tried to talk her out of it,
but she lies and says she only smokes a little bit.
She was my friend,
but now she's not,
because then I found out that she now takes pot.

Laura Rushton (11) Beechwood Primary School

MY FRIEND

My friend is the best,
She surely beats the rest,
She will always be a part,
of my beating heart.
We have been through grief together,
We shall always be friends forever.
She loves a good laugh,
But that's not half!
She is my best friend,
I hope we'll be friends to the end.

Jane Squires (11) Beechwood Primary School

DOGS

Black, white, brown and grey,
It's my turn to feed today.

Meaty chunks
Is a healthy lunch.

When smells the food
He's in a mood.

Gobbles it up
He's now full up.

Postman's mad
But dog is glad.

I'm about to start a race
He licks me in the face.

I wrestle him in bed
Because he sleeps above my head.

Samantha Mancey (10) Beechwood Primary School

A FISHY FRIEND

A little fish went to look
In every cranny and nook
He said to his friend
'Will this be my end?
For here comes a fisherman's hook.'

Louise Proctor (10) Beechwood Primary School

CHEWING GUM

I know a little rascal
his real name is Fred,
and once he flicked,
some chewing gum
it landed on my head.
That night I tried to
get it out I guess
I had no luck. I really,
really wish it wasn't
really stuck. The next
day at school it was
assembly in the hall.
When little Fred came
up to me and said
'Have you still got my
old chewing gum in your head.

Louise Pegg (10) Beechwood Primary School

GYM

Gym, gym it's a wonderful
sport,
but sometimes you need a bit of
support.
There's the bar, vault, floor and
beam,
but they're not easy as they may
seem.
Practice makes perfect,
so I am told
if you want to go for number 1
    Gold!

Rachel Bowker (11) Beechwood Primary School

SADNESS

Sadness is a little boy on his
own in the corner.

Sadness is a funeral when
someone is dead.

Sadness is one boy's mum and dad
when they fight and argue.

Sadness is one person's nightmare.

Sadness is being on your own in
the cold.

Sadness is one boy being bullied
by those who don't care.

Christopher Rich (11) Beechwood Primary School

LONELINESS

It was playtime.
I was alone.
It felt miserable.
I was by myself at the
corner of the playground all
alone.
I felt paralysed, I looked
at the children
Playing.
They didn't like me
I was sure.
The bell rang.
The children ran in,
I walked.

Michael Williams (10) Beechwood Primary School

THE WORLD

Travel to a far off place.
Where you'll never see a friendly face.
A place called earth where people die.
A place that's trashed and people cry.
Someone's lonely, no one cares.
There's no fish, bees, birds or bears.

Nature, nature everywhere.
And loneliness is trapped in there.
A place of joy and happiness
A place that no longer is a mess.
Someone cries, someone dies
We rush over there because we care.

The two worlds are the same.
What a shame, what a shame
One is of death and war
And the other's of friends where no one's sore
Where's the peace, where's the fun
Where's the evil that killed everyone

Hayley Cowcher (11) Beechwood Primary School

SCORPION

It's sly, silent, shiny, slippery,
secret and sickening.
It swipes and stings, snips,
and snaps.

Tom Hartnell (11) Beechwood Primary School

THE FUN FAIR

Children, children everywhere, children, children here and there.
On the go-carts on the ghost train. On the roller coaster, a kiddies funfair boaster.
Eating candyfloss, hot dogs, burgers and different foods.

Children, children everywhere, children, children here and there.
Round and round they do go, getting dizzy on the tea pot ride.
Spending parents a fortune at the great funfair, but us cool kids do not care. Winning prizes on different games, getting scared on dark ghost trains.

Nikki Macedo (10) Beechwood Primary School

THE DUMP

There once was a boy who had so much hair
That he looked like a woolly bear.
He cut off his hair
Until his head was bare.
He bought a wig
That was a bit big.
He thought it would be a hit.
So he wore it.
His friends thought he'd committed a sin
So they put him in the bin.
He got collected by the dustman,
And taken in a rubbish van
To a dump
Situated at Chiddely-bump.
He crawled out and ran about,
Until he got run over by a car.

Neil Warlow (10) Beechwood Primary School

THE BOY IN JAIL

There was a boy in jail
And nobody could afford his bail.
He was in jail, because he cut off
a dog's tail.
And then he slipped on some ale.
He hit his head on a wall,
and he started to call.
A policeman came up and said,
What are you doing son?
But the boy ran past,
and hit him on the tum.

Nick Birch (11) Beechwood Primary School

TREES

Trees suddenly burst into life
They're a home for insects and birds,
And they whistle in the wind.

A gentle dancer blowing about,
But other times they are still,
They are beautiful for hammocks

They are tall and graceful,
Brilliant for tree-houses,
And are full of bugs

After blossoming in the spring,
They have pure green leaves for summer,
Then comes autumn a beautiful sight,
Red, golden and dark green leaves,
Now is winter, where's all his clothes
gone?

Sarah Squires (11) Beechwood Primary School

BIRTHDAY PARTY

All excited,
Friends arrive,
Giving presents,
All alive.

Dancing dancing,
On your feet,
Ending soon,
Time to eat.

Food galore,
Biscuits and cake,
Chocolate, strawberry,
Banana milk shake.

All the rubbish,
Thrown away,
Then we play games,
For the rest of the day.

Friends all go,
Party end,
Then up the stairs,
Slowly ascend.

Time for bed,
Very sleepy,
Going . . . going . . . goin . . . go . . . g . . .

In the morning,
All is lighted,
Friends arrive,
Very excited.

Rhiannon Phillips (10) Beechwood Primary School

REMEMBRANCE

R emember the people that die
E ven in your memory
M ums dads even children die
E verybody loses someone
M any people die in wars
B e brave forget the past
E very day people die
R emember in your memory all the time you had
   with them

Kim O'Reilly (11) Beechwood Primary School

REMEMBRANCE VE DAY

The war the war
It was terrible and sore
All the soldiers who went to fight
Wasted away in the night
Spitfires firing!
Bombs exploding everywhere
The enemies did not care!
All the people had a scare
Children being evacuated here and
there
6 years of people crying
Everybody is dying
In the end Europe won
The war is now over and done
Street parties everywhere!

Laura Serafin (10) Beechwood Primary School

THE PRISON

School is a prison
School is boring
School means *science* in the morning.

Get up, get dressed
Oh, where's my vest?
Who wants school to be the best?

Register, oh here it comes
If we're late he'll click our thumbs.

Oh no, I'm late,
Ouch ouch ouch!
It didn't hurt all that much
I didn't know he had such
Stupid rules.

Ding ding ding
There's the bell
We're last today
Oh hell oh hell!

After lunch,
Munch munch munch
Silent reading
What a crunch.

Now it's maths, my favourite subject
Not really
But nearly.

It's home time now
Yes yes yes.
Home time is my subject best
'Hi mum I had the worst day ever'
'How about we go out together?'
'Yeah!'

Vikki Aust (10) Beechwood Primary School

THE BULLY

A knuckle clicking
Nose picking
Ear twisting
Threat resisting
Name calling
Hair pulling,
Bruises aching,
We start shaking,
He starts grinning
We know he's winning
At last, the end of break.

Cathy Stoter (11) Beechwood Primary School

I REMEMBER THE WAR

I remember walking through all the mud.
I remember hearing all the gun fire.
I remember dodging all the bombs.
I remember all my friends being shot or bombed.
I remember getting caught in the barbed wire.
I remember watching all the planes being blown up.
I remember hearing the sirens
I remember holding a gun
I remember the air raid shelters.
I remember black outs
I remember shooting Germans
I remember it all on VE Day.

James Reynolds (11) Beechwood Primary School

THE SHARK

A swift swimmer,
A deadly hunter,
A flesh ripper,
A wave skipper.

A fish eater,
An enemy beater,
A strong fighter,
A merciless killer.

Claire Gowler (11) Beechwood Primary School

TIME IS RACING BY

Time goes by
Slowly, surely,
Fast, speeding,
Cruising round.

The hands are racing round the clock.
The time goes by
Tic-tac-tock.

You can't teach a teacher new tricks
So stop wasting your time.
Get on down to your work,
Stop acting like a jerk.

The hands are racing round the clock.
The time goes by
Tic-tac-tock.
The hands are racing round the clock.
The time goes by
Tic-tac-tock.

Tick tick tick
      Time!

Katie Bell (11) Beechwood Primary School

SALLY

I remember
Mum and I used to take
My dog for a walk
When I was four.

I remember
I used to go to sleep
In her basket
When I was five.

When I was six at school
I cried for my dog.
Because I loved her
So much.

I remember Sally and I would run
Around the garden
And play football
And after that we would lie in the grass.

I remember,
When I didn't eat my dinner
Putting it under the table
And she would eat it for me.

I remember
When Sally died unexpectedly
She was lying in her bed
Both eyes open, I cried.

I'll always remember
My dog Sally.

Robert Dean (10) Beechwood Primary School

REMEMBRANCE

British soldiers keep on trying
Even though they keep on dying.
Bombs and shells blowing up
Everything in their path.
Bombers, Spitfires, every plane,
Killing millions all the time.

Jonathan Norton-Standen (10) Beechwood Primary School

THE WAR

Turn those lights off.
Keep the curtains closed.
Close those doors.
All those soldiers that went to fight far away
Soldiers wasted away by the day.
Remember, remember those soldiers who went out to
                      fight for our country
Children were evacuated.
People were crying and dying.
In the end the war lasted six years.
At last the war had ended.
Street parties were thrown
Cheers were all over Europe
Europe had won.

Melanie-Jayne Radburn (10) Beechwood Primary School

MY RABBIT DIED

M y nan buried Poppy, she said
Y ou can always get a new

R abbit you know, yes but what
A bout Poppy, my very own rabbit who's
B uried in the
B ack garden
I feel sad when I
T hink of her

Victoria Crombie (10) Beechwood Primary School

REMEMBRANCE

Furry and soft,
Black as night.
My grandma's cat was a beautiful sight,
Hurrying, scurrying on the lawn,
Sometimes even at dawn!
Purring and sleeping by the fire,
She climbed trees, higher and higher,
So we all remember,
Grandma's lovely cat,
Remember her lying on the really soft mat.

Francesca Carrisi (10) Beechwood Primary School

REMEMBRANCE

R is for raid.
E is for enemy.
M is for more deaths.
E is for evacuation.
M is for more gun shooting.
B is for the Blitz.
R is for rotting bodies.
A is for anti aircraft guns.
N is for nurses.
C is for cruelty.
E is for escape.

Michael Halpin (10) Beechwood Primary School

FRED THE MOUSE

F red was my first pet mouse
R ed eyes and white fur
E very day I would feed him fruit
D ead Fred is now in heaven
        I hope he is happy there.

T he day he died I was upset and sad
H e was the best pet I've ever had
E very day I would hold him and
        play with him.

M eat was Fred's favourite food
O n Fred's hamster wheel Fred would play
U nder Fred's sawdust Fred would hide
S mall Fred was, but he was a good friend
E very time I think of Fred I feel a bit sad.

Matthew Walsha (10) Beechwood Primary School

UNTITLED

It's dark outside it's blackout time
No light to be seen
Not even a crack
Everything sealed tight
Not again tonight

The siren sounds the sky's ablaze
There are planes all around
There are planes above in the search light's maze
Out of bed and to the shelter we must go
What ever the weather rain or snow

It's morning time, time for school no school
Till noon that's the rule
Since all clear sounded after midnight
Till noon of day we can all sleep tight.
Loaded down school bag
Gas mask too my shoulders are free of tension
All we now fear is sheer detention

Peter Brown (10) Beechwood Primary School

REMEMBRANCE

R emembrance.
E urope is independent.
M emories bad.
E urope has victory.
M any people die.
B ombs no longer drop.
R etreating Germans.
A fter 6 years of war VE Day.
N azis defeated.
C oming home.
E verybody happy.

Chris Jones (10) Beechwood Primary School

REMEMBRANCE OF THE WAR

At the start of the war I heard people screaming
At the end of the war I heard people cheering
In the Blitz bombs came down
Which made everybody rush under ground,
In the night no lights glowing
German bombs keep on bombing.
In the day people crying
British soldiers keep on trying.
Even if Hitler's winning
After all the war's just beginning.
Six years of sadness
Just because of someone's madness.
So let's remember all the people
As they fell to the ground,
Trying to bring peace to the land.

Lee Cowcher (10) Beechwood Primary School

REMEMBRANCE

R emember the war painful and sore.
E very child is evacuated to safety.
M any lives were lost. Be thankful
      for the people who fought in the war for us.
E ndless fighting and bombing
M any dads sent to the war.
B e careful you never know just in case
      Nazi bombs might be blowing.
R iots going on everywhere.
A fraid to move or even turn the light on.
C onfused faces watch bombs.
E verybody is thankful that the
      war is over and done with.

Chris Blackall (10) Beechwood Primary School

DO YOU REMEMBER THE WAR?

Do you remember the war?
People dying rich and poor
Do you remember the war?
People with wounds septic and sore
People dying for all of us
So that's why there's so much fuss
Bombs falling down and down
People hiding underground
When they came up and looked around
There's bombs and shells scattered on the ground

No more ration books
No more Blitz
No more blackouts
No more *war!*

Claire Carter (11) Beechwood Primary School

THE BLACK CAT

I see him in the sunlight,
Walking to the tall meadow,
Playing with his girlfriend,
Jumping the tally shady grass,
Playing hide and seek with his mate,
I see him pounce on a little old brown mouse,
Digging a hole and burying the mouse
Kissing his girlfriend again,
Walking up a hill.
I see him in the moonlight,
Then I say goodbye, goodbye,
OK black cat.

Kerri Mack (11) Brightwalton CE Primary School

MARBLE

Hard and cold, smooth and shiny,
White and sparkling,
Smells salty,
No taste.
Glittering lustre.

Michelle Drennan (9) Brightwalton CE Primary School

THE MAGIC ON A SPRING DAY

The blossom on the tree is like pink
snowballs in the air.
The muddy brown bulbs like magic change
To beautiful red and yellow tulips.
Grass, wet and green with the morning dew;
The fresh, sweet scent of the spring air;
The ground: white with daisies.
Sometimes a yellow dot where
dandelions lie.

Charlotte Clarke (9) Brightwalton CE Primary School

AMETHYST QUARTZ

Quartz! A pretty, dazzling sight;
Look at it shining and glistening in the moonlight,
Or sparkling in the sunlight;
Touch it - ow! It's sharp and pointed,
Rough and scratchy.

Emily Clarke (11) Brightwalton CE Primary School

MINERALS

Agate:
Bright colourful colours of the rainbow,
It is like the salty sea,
The perfumed oranges of the tree.
It is like a piece of smooth glass
Calcite:
Clear
It also feels like a piece of smooth glass
Glittering in the moonlight;
Colourful bright rainbow in the calcite
It is like the falling rain
In the blue tinkling sky.
Hard and stiff like a slice of metal.

Lottie Beaumont (8) Brightwalton CE Primary School

WAR HORSE

One sunny day,
I sat on some hay,
In a big green field of grass,
And there in the distance,
I saw something glisten,
In the light of the sun.

Then galloping towards me,
As big as a sycamore tree,
Was a horse in shining armour,
As he got closer I could hear his thundering hooves,
Pounding the ground like the comets that fall from
the sky.

He slowed to a walk and approached me,
He looked at me with big, brown eyes,
And out of his mouth he produced,
A sword, a shield and armour,
I picked them up with pride,
Then mounted his armoured back,

      And off we rode to
      war.

Anna Wise (10) Caversham Primary School

BACK TO SCHOOL

Back to school
Back to school
I just don't want to go back to school!
More and more maths and
                        G
                        E
                        O
                        G
                        R
                        A
                        P
                        H
                        Y
                        !
               Just endless history and mystery!

Teachers say no! And teachers say yes. Try to get them going the *right* way!
Why don't you leave it and go out to play!
Children get hurt and children start crying!
Bullies push and punch, little 'uns who are whining, with dread!
    I
       just
           wish
               I
                   could
                       stay
                           and
                              curl
up in bed!

So that is the story of my school!
Whether it's nice or whether it's cool! Whether
I shall curl myself up in my bed
Or whether I should go to school instead!

Lucy Claire Hounsom (9) Crazies Hill CE School

SEA SIDE WASH-UPS

Things that wash-up on my toes pretty stones and cockle shells.
The sea turns around and flows back in to the huge ocean.

Bad things that wash-up on the rocks clothes and old socks.
Bitter litter and rotten wood aren't good.

Sea shells everywhere wash-up once but stay there.
Pick them up and take them home.
Listen to the sea rushing in and out all alone.

Victoria Cope (9) Crazies Hill CE School

THE FIELD MOUSE

There is an old owl, who sits in a tree,
A funny old owl who keeps looking for me;
For I am a field mouse so brave and so free,
That's why I live at the base of a tree.

For I have a small family of four
And my house has a front and a back door.
Now I must feed my family of four,
I need to go for my nightly tour.

As I scamper into the night
The owl will watch me with most delight.
For if I was to freeze he'll put to flight.
And then I will become his meal for the night.

Tammie Hiscock (11) Crazies Hill CE School

THE SCARECROW

The scarecrow lives in the field,
His coat is old and torn,
He's lonely and cold all winter,
In the summer he's lovely and warm.

The farmer hangs tins on the
Scarecrow to keep the birds off
His crop,
But when the wind isn't blowing
The birds eat the lot!
They like the scarecrow.
And are not frightened of him,
When they are busy eating
He always gives them a grin.

Kelley Hiscock (9) Crazies Hill CE School

GREEN

G reen is peaceful

R each up help the ozone

E vergreen forests

E den the garden of life

N ature worlds best source.

Zoe Brooker (9) Crazies Hill CE School

SUZIE'S SLEEPOVER

Suzie's friends are over to stay,
They're not sleeping they're going to play,
Chocolate,
Popcorn,
Ice cream,
Cake,
Fudge and toffee,
Cadbury's flake.
Kate is sleepy ready to dream
But Jenny's just started on the toffee ice
Cream.
Charlotte and Alice are talking like mad,
'Great said Suzie this party ain't bad.'

Joanne Hendry (10) Crazies Hill CE School

SLIP BUMP CRASH

I went ice skating
with all my friends
we had a great time,
the fun never ends!
I fell over and bumped my head
'You're a bit silly' my mum said!
Talking as usual laughing away
we forgot there were other people trying to play!
And we all went *Slip! Bump! Crash!*
That was the *best ever* birthday bash!

Louisa Sidery (10) Crazies Hill CE School

THE FINAL FRONTIER

Space is called the final frontier,
The subject of stories, legend and lore,
Astronauts fly into space,
To batter at the frontier.
But the final frontier is firmly fixed.
And really nothing but a mix,
Of planets' scientists all over the universe,
All in union to batter down the frontier.
But of other planets Earth knows nothing.
And so we must let the broken frontier slip,
Into a dream,
Of Hi-Tech machines,
And wake, into the knowledge that,
The final frontier is ever here.

Ian E S Higgins (11) *Courthouse Junior School*

SPRING

Daffodils are blooming,
Frogs are laying spawn,
All is bright and sunny,
All is bright and warm.
A beautiful carpet of daisies,
Spring is here.

Blossom is coming out,
Petals falling like confetti,
Carpeting the ground,
When the gentle wind blows,
Spring is here.

Amy Lyczba (10) *Courthouse Junior School*

THE HIGHWAY MAN

I wander aimlessly through the thicket
In my belt I have two pistols
I crouch in some grass
It is a warm night
In the distance I hear a stage coach rumbling
along the road.
An owl hoots its cries echoing all around
The stage coach draws nearer
I get ready to jump out
I shoot my pistol in the air, *bang*
Two horses rear up and stop
With one fatal shot I shoot the driver dead!
'Empty your pockets' I shout
The man and wife empty their pockets
I grab all of the jewels and gold coins and run
into the field
Stop and sit
Later I hear whistles
'Come out in the name of the law'
I panic but that doesn't help, I'm caught
In my head I hear a boom now it's time to
face my doom.

Kiran Sinhal (11) Courthouse Junior School

THE POSH HORSE

There it was a beautiful grey
Cantering along the green cross bay,
Its head was held high
Its ears were forward and its mane was
Blowing in the wind,
It stopped suddenly and looked at me
And cantered away again.

Julie-Ann Allen (11) Courthouse Junior School

A NEW PUPPY

Dad said I could get a new puppy
So I hopped into the car
And strained my neck to the front seat
And asked him 'Is it far'

We got to the puppy home
And saw the puppies there
They barked and squealed and wriggled on
Until we took one to our care.

A shiny golden Labrador
With quite becoming eyes
And extremely floppy ears
And a mouth that always sighs.

Emma Hill (11) Courthouse Junior School

THE HOUSE IN THE WOODS

The house in the wood was a horrible sight.
Bricks and tiles falling down in the night.
I entered inside and the rain came down
And on my face put a worried frown.

Up the creaking stairs to an opened door.
A floorboard gave way and I fell to the floor.
I ran down the stairs and out of the door
Through the woods until I felt secure.

Joel Stacey (11) Courthouse Junior School

PUSHING AND SHOVING

Pushing and shoving.
They never stop.
It's early Saturday morning in town.
We go to the cafe.
But it's even worse there.
I went to the sports shop.
I nearly got trampled there.
Went to Tescos got hit by a trolley.
Kids were screaming bread went flying.
Mums were shouting.
Pushing and shoving.
We ran outside
Away from it all.
Into the shoe shop.
Shop assistants rushing running around.
They're even worse
We quickly ran out into the street.
Back to the car
Going home at last.
Away from it all.

Leah Bowers (11) Courthouse Junior School

THE SUN AND THE SKY

Not a cloud in the sky,
only the sun's twinkle in my eye.
it shines so bright with all its mighty light.
up so high beyond the sky into space what a place.

I like the summer because my mother
takes me on trips, down the river to the zoo
and then on the the new leisure pool.

I like the sun it's fun.

Andrew Collins (11) Courthouse Junior School

SPRING

Spring, spring is here at last
The time didn't come very fast.
I have been waiting all year round
Little flowers come out of the ground
Daisies, dandelions and daffodils.

In spring you play all day
Hoping it will never go away.
So spring is here - come and
See the flowers
Daisies, dandelions and daffodils.

Sarah Haunton (10) Courthouse Junior School

FACTORY WORKING

I work in a factory all day long
I hope when I am fifteen I am gone
From this cruel and disgusting place,
where we only make lace,
for a rich lady with a grin on her face
I'll run away one day at a tremendous pace
I'm the one that will be coming back
with a grin on my face
For I'll have a factory that makes lace.

Hannah Hunt (10) Courthouse Junior School

I WORK IN A MILL

I work in a mill,
And I work for twelve hours a day,
You don't get much pay,
You move out the way,
If you want to stay,
In the factory.

I want to run away,
And never come back,
But if I did I would get the sack,
And if I fall asleep I get a whack,
I do it for my family,
So we don't have to pack,
I have to keep working,
In the factory.

I get so dirty,
That you wouldn't believe,
You wouldn't get dirty if you weave,
My dad works in the mill with me,
And there is so much smoke,
That you can't see,
When you work,
In the factory.

Rachel Garland (10) Courthouse Junior School

SPRING

S pring is here, time for
P laying in the sun. The
R ising of the sun early,
I n the morning. Daffodils
N eatly swaying in the breeze
G lorious spring is here again

Louise McCarthy (10) Courthouse Junior School

DAFFODILS

Their brightly coloured
petals show out in a glow.
The daffodils arise from soil below
their stalks tall and thin.
Dancing like ballerinas in the wind.
Their trumpets like a bright star
in the night sky
At last they are free in
beautiful spring.

Michelle Henry (10) Courthouse Junior School

SIGNS OF SPRING

Frog spawn in the pond
Daffodils growing strong
The nights get short
And the days are long

The eggs in nests hatch
Birds chirp with pride
Flowers and grass grow over
the hills
In our fabulous countryside

Crocuses bloom and buds appear
Making our world loud and bright
A gentle breeze swoops along
Revealing the sun's glamorous
light.

Jenny Mathieson (9) Courthouse Junior School

SPRING FLOWERS

Winter honeysuckle is
opening,
Grape hyacinths sway in the sun
Up come the bulbs of daffodils
Spring has begun.

Bluebells open and happily sing
Daisies play till the day is done
Hawthorns open bright new leaves
Spring has begun.

Primroses grow golden
Celandines shine clear
To bring the happy sunshine
Spring is here!

Louise Jell (10) Courthouse Junior School

A WINTER EVENING

In the cold frosty evening everything is still,
The trees calm and serene,
Bright rosy skies framing a scarlet sun,
The world bright and ethereal.

The ground blanketed with an ivory carpet,
Everything a glinting,
Everywhere dazzling with exquisite patterns;
A shimmering picture twinkling with frost.

The trees stark and bare,
Black and brooding,
A man comes trudging with a boy and a sled,
Now the virgin snow spoiled by footprints.

Emily Noden (10) Courthouse Junior School

THE YOUNG AND OLD RIVERS

YOUNG RIVER

Like a swift eagle hunting its prey.
Like a violent express train rattling on its sidings.
A young hooligan looking for excitement.
A young untrained puppy dog dashing and rushing about.
Like vibrant young disco dancers raving all night.
A young infantile boy running to the sweet shop.
A frisky lamb waiting for some food.
Like a flash Jaguar going for a test drive.

OLD RIVER

An old gentleman dawdling slowly along the street.
An old sock worn at the heel.
A lazy, heavy cargo train trying to pull its load.
An old plodding elephant without a care in the world.
Like a calm old river boat paddling through the water
Like an unhurried vintage car driving along the road.
Like a ripped, tatty book lying on the shelf.

Gary Jacklin (10) & Luke Baxter (10) Courthouse Junior School

THE FLYING SCOTSMAN

There's nothing so fine as driving a train.
I even go in wind and rain.
With a toot from my whistle.
And a honk from my horn.
It'll keep me going till the day is born.
With soot in my hair and smoke in my eyes.
That's the way that time flies.

I look outside and what do I see.
I see a family of one, two, three.
I see a stream it looks so near.
That fresh water so lovely and clear.
As I lean out of the window there's wind in my face.
I love to be standing in this place.

I smell the smoke as it enters the air.
Where are we going?
I don't know where.
We're nearly there we've had some fun.
Toot toot! My work is done.

Tom Wallis (10) Courthouse Junior School

A WINTER SCENE

The bleak, calm wind whispers
Through the hedgerows in the early evening.
The stark, broad trunk of a leafless tree
Drains away into slender branches.
The silence is deafening
But for a small robin chirping.
The thawing snow glints
In the last ray of sunlight.
A slight gloomy mist casts a murky shadow
Over the rest of the garden.
The blues and oranges, reds and yellows
Blend into each other to reveal a dazzling sunset.
Silhouettes of birds emerge on the sunset,
The last few birds to migrate.

I trudge along, all on my own,
Out to capture the winter scene.

Samantha Richards (11) Courthouse Junior School

A WINTER STORM

Lifeless plants wearily drooping on the ground,
The bleak wind nipping at your ears,
The murky sky overcast by the stormy clouds,
The silhouette of naked trees darkened by the misty sky,
The perfect carpet of white snow starts to gleam as
A glimmer of light bursts through the misty clouds,
The whole earth seems to lighten up,
The silhouettes of trees turn to miraculous rich brown colours,
The ice begins to shine like a wonderful mirror,
The wind suddenly drops and the world is silent,
The storm is over!

Hamish Harris (11) Courthouse Junior School

A CAT'S LIFE

She lies in the warm sun,
Stretched out on the wall,
Without a care in the world.
Her black fur gleaming,
Her eyes firmly closed,
but now and then she has a little peep
to see what's going on.
She thinks about the days gone by,
The days when she was with her family.
She tries hard to dream about when she was
young, it seems like only yesterday,
Her sisters were around her and
her mother's tender tongue was
Licking her gently.

Charlotte Rumble (11) Courthouse Junior School

THE GENTLE RIVER

Comes from the Alm,
Down to the pasture.
Peaceful and calm,
Comes from its master.
Peacefully trickling,
Pebbles it's tickling.
Into the valley,
The river will run.
Rolling and swirling,
Twisting and turning,
Dipping and diving,
And intertwining.
Looking so pretty,
Handsome and witty,
Falling so trickly,
Down from the Alm . . .
Gracefully meandering,
Bubbling and swirling,
Twisting and turning,
Your gentle trickle.
Happily travelling
Bibbling and babbling
Whirling and swirling
Down the mountainside.

Christiane Jell (11) Courthouse Junior School

GALLOPING

Galloping, galloping over the sand,
Galloping, galloping wind sweeps the land.
The time is dawn in the morning light,
Splashing waves, feels like flight.

Cantering, cantering on a grass verge,
Cantering, cantering the power, the urge.
The sun shines brightly, lights the sky,
Sniffing the freshly made hay.

Trotting, trotting, around a field,
Trotting, trotting so happy I feel.
My riding time it is almost up,
Slowing, walking, then dead stop.

Lara Easton (11) Courthouse Junior School

SUMMER TIME

The summer sand falls through my hand,
While I'm playing on the beach.
The sun beats down, it's midday,
The sun's heat is at its peak.
The waves are calm, a few white horses are
Frolicking in the waves.
The gulls are soaring,
My dad is snoring,
While my mother and brother get us ice-creams.
The donkey rides are on the side of the beach,
They are having races, while they shout with joy.
After the race when nobody cares who's won,
There is a smile upon all their faces,
Then up goes the shout -
    Can we have another go?

Rosie Heath (11) Courthouse Junior School

THE FLOWER

Flowers, flowers are so bright
    The sun light shines on the petals
        Blue, pink and yellow
            All the colours you could
                wish for.
And all the different types of flowers
    Poppies, roses and pansies
        They fill the garden with
            all kinds of smells.

Gemma Taylor (11) Courthouse Junior School

THE SNAIL

As the snail moves slowly
onward leaving a silvery line
behind him.
It twinkles in the night's light.
It must be heavy having to carry
that shell on his back but he
manages somehow.
The shell is sometimes useful
when it snows or rains.
The little snail just curls up
inside his pretty patterned home.
When the rain or snow has stopped
he pops his head out of his little
home.
First his antenna, followed by his body
and tail.
The little snail sets off again on his
travels leaving a silvery trail.

Layla Stevenson (10) Courthouse Junior School

COUNTRYSIDE

The countryside where the crops grow.
Where the birds fly and the streams flow.
The crops grow side by side where the field
mice try to hide.

A boiling tractor grunts by, complaining about
the hot summer sky.

The sheep crawls into the shade trying to
escape the hot summer's blade.
The horses gallop through the field. The pony
using its parents as a shield.

The summer plants start to grow the colourful
petals start to show,
The night is coming and the wind and rain
but tomorrow it will be the same again.

Jonathan Stuart (11) Courthouse Junior School

WYCOMBE WANDERERS FOOTBALL CLUB

Wycombe, Wycombe the boys in blue,
Wycombe, Wycombe we love you.
From the Conference to Division Two,
Wycombe, Wycombe we love you.
Cousins in defence and Hyde in goal,
And McGavin playing the striker's role.
Terry Evans strong and tall,
We will always win the ball.
Keith Ryan was one of the best,
But he got injured and had to rest.
Wycombe finished the season on a high,
And sent Leyton Orient bye, bye, bye . . .

Richard Price (11) Courthouse Junior School

PLAYING FOR MY DREAM TEAM

It was my debut
For the football club Man U.
I was in the tunnel,
nervous as can be
The wild crowd
was towering over me.
I went for the ball
The victim experienced a nasty fall.
And crunch!
The man threw a nasty punch.
The crowd was ecstatic
The fellow on the floor was rather dramatic.
Their team was defending
Then I released a shot that was bending.
Goal! Goal! I leapt with joy
Alex Ferguson called me a good boy.

James Hawkes (11) Courthouse Junior School

LIFE

Daylight's fading,
Night draws in.
We're all cosy,
Drinking gin.

Time for bed now,
Snug and warm.
Sleeping till,
A new day's born.

Now it's daylight,
Sun comes out.
Spreading bright new,
Light about.

Sarah Jennings (11) Churchend Primary School

BORING OLD SCHOOL!

The alarm clock rings as loud as could be
I don't want to go to school I just want to be free
After I'm dressed it's off downstairs I go,
To eat some soggy cereal . . . Oh no!
Now it's time to brush my hair,
There's so many knots, it's not fair.
Then it's time to go to school,
Boy do I feel so uncool.
                Boring old school!

We start the day off with assembly
The headmaster tries to be friendly
Assembly is a great big bore
So everybody starts to snore.
At last it's time to go out to play
But it's not our turn on the adventure playground today
Then we have to go in,
And have a roaring old sing
Then it's time to have some lunch,
I've got water but I'd rather have punch.
Now it's time for school to end
And a letter I will send . . .
To complain,
Because I think they're all insane!
                Boring old school
                Boring old school!

Shoshana Ross (11) Churchend Primary School

THE DANCE OF THE DOLPHINS

As I sit on the dusty sand
I watch the still quiet water
The moon shines brightly what a wonderful sight
It lights up the calm blue sea.

And then the beautiful show begins
The grey animals jump and sing
They are called dolphins, dolphins they are called.

Then I see them fading away
Into the calm horizon,
One day I think I will see them again.
Nobody knows what happens when they dance and
Sing
In the calm moonlight.

Carly Burke (11) Churchend Primary School

RABBITS

Rabbits running rustling in the grass,
Trying to go ever so fast,
Getting wet under the tree
There they go all in a three.

Our rabbit loves to be free,
He runs in the garden so happily.

Our pet rabbit is here to stay,
Nice and warm on a cold winter's day,
Running around,
Trying not to make a sound.

He hates being put away,
So he tries outside to stay,
He can't stay for foxes might come,
Then he'll have to run.

Danielle Cserfalvi (10) Churchend Primary School

STRAWBERRIES

Down behind the big oak tree,
Grows fruit, red as can be
Crunchy, a bit sweet,
Also tangy and petite
The strawberries at the bottom of the garden.

Shiny and bobbly on the outside,
Delicious with cream.
Too tasty to hide
Behind the big oak tree.

Flowers appear
As the strawberries die off,
Of that scrumptious red fruit,
I could never have enough,
Down behind the big oak tree.

Sarah Wanklyn (11) Crown Wood School

GOING SHOPPING

Potato chips, cherries, coconuts and sweets,
Ketchup and fish, choc ices and treats.
Beans, peas, butter and cheese,
Would you like a milk shake.
Yes please,
Yoghurt, chocolate, burgers and jam.
Would you like milk or a can and ham,
Let's go shopping again,
And choose some more food.
Would you like that,
Yes I would,
Oh good.

Natalie Wright (11) Crown Wood School

DIFFERENCES

There's a real big difference between black and white,
A difference to be taught between wrong and right.

If every person in the world was the same,
Not one person had a different name,
How would the world cope with everyone,
No different habits like sucking your thumb.
I bet every person reading this feels the same
Without differences the world would be lame.

Yet people criticise skin colour black from white,
It's not their fault. There's no wrong from right.
Who can imagine a world with no night or day?
I just prefer the world this way!

Samantha Brown (11) Crown Wood School

THE RUNAWAY TRAIN

The runaway train goes
down the hill,

Choo choo as it scutters
along the rails,

Faster and faster as it
picks up speed,

The train goes flying
into the reeds.

The passengers get out
safe and sound,

The driver ends up in
a local town.

David Bird (10) Crown Wood School

MY MAGIC BOX

I will put in my box . . .
A sharp gleam of sunlight
And the lights from its rays
The hairs of a caterpillar
And a song of praise.

My box will be made out of . . .
Star and moonlight
And the seas so clear and bright
My box will have a glittering star
And the roaring of a motor car.

I will use my box to love and care . . .
And to help each other share.
I will give people some of the gold,
That my lovely box does hold
Because my box is big and bold.

Jessica Ballyntine (10) Crown Wood School

ANIMALS

Animals animals everywhere,
Dolphins cows and whales everywhere,
Some are kind some are cruel,
But I love them all.
How much fun they can be too
Reptiles mammals as well,
Lions and tigers are dangerous.
Animals in danger have got to be
Saved, in case they get extinct,
So try to save.

Heather Fernley (10) Crown Wood School

MY BOX OF MAGIC

I will put in my box,
The last day of sun,
A tube full of fun,
And the feeling you get,
When you have just won.

The first cry of a baby,
Just been born,
The smell that you get,
After mowing the lawn.

My box would be made
Of a wood never seen,
It would not be square
But tall and lean,
The lock would only open
For someone to see,
If that person wished
To see the dreams made by me.

Rachel Wilkinson (11) Crown Wood School

WAVING AT TRAINS

I like to wave at trains
as they hurry down the track
but when I stick my tongue out,
nobody waves back.

Christina Butchers (10) Crown Wood School

FORESTS AND FLOWERS

As I walk through the forest
I see the flowers and the trees
The bluebells and the grass
Stand beneath the trees

As I walk through the forest
I see dandelion whose stems are
Spring green that stand in the
Grass beneath the old oak tree

As I walk through the forest
I see nests one, two, three,
Up in the branches of the old
ash tree.

As I walk through the forest
I see the flowers and the bees
All making honey for our lovely teas.

Wendy Brown (10) Crown Wood School

MOUNTAINS

      Up in the mountains
where it's cold and icy
The snow drips because of the sun
Feel the cold wind blowing on
hands.
      Don't look down unless you
want to fall.
      Night time comes you're still
climbing look at the moon.
Look at it shining.

Hollie Brightman (10) Crown Wood School

MANCHESTER UNITED, TAKING THE MICK

Peter Schmeichel should be called
Michael then his two names would rhyme.

Paul Parker comes out when it's darker
because he only plays night games.

Denis Irwin keeps occurring when they've
got a free kick.

Steve Bruce hates orange juice
and his favourite holiday place is Toulouse.

Lee Sharpe likes catching carp.

Gary Pallister holds up a banister
saying, 'Don't tackle me I'm too scared!'

Eric Cantona hates Yeboah because
he plays for Leeds!

Paul Ince is made of mince!

Brian Mclair don't half like
a chocolate eclair.

Mark Hughes takes on number twos
and scores (and they have number twos)

Ryan Giggs wears loads of wigs!
(Don't know how he's got lots of girlfriends then)

David May loves his pay day.
(Gets paid enough too doesn't he)

Gary Walsh loves his Porche.

Andrei Kanchelskis slipped a disc
trying to twist and turn.
(Well, he is a winger of course)

Roy Keane is so mean
because he ate a runner bean.

Andy Cole is Old King Cole
because he always scores a vital goal.

Gary Neville is a bit of a devil
and so is his brother Phil!
(Phillip Neville, brother of Gary), Manchester U.

Lee Avery (11) Crown Wood School

SEEING A BIRD

Out of my window,
over there,
I see a Robin with,
fair brown hair,
It is sitting on a bench,
whistling away,
Oh my what a lovely day.

Someone came along,
and scared the robin,
Away,
come back Robin,
On a sunny day,

It was a Monday,
morning,
I saw the Robin again,
it flew right on to my,
Windowsill,
and started whistling,
Again,
Fly away Robin,
high up in the sky,
Don't come back until,
summer in July.

Amy Gillard (11) Crown Wood School

THE MOORS OVER YORKSHIRE

Over the moors see the stars,
In the wood see the animals,
In the morning see the sunshine gapes,
With a lot of colours in the sky,
See the sun shine mist
Hear the Yorkshire birds
Look at the grass it's just like crystal in the moors,
Drive by the lake see the sunshine against the
Fish,
Hear the old fashioned train listen to the way
It goes up the hill it's gasping for air,
When the night comes
Go fast asleep.

Terri Lochyer (11) Crown Wood School

DRAGON

Beware my teeth are like knives,
My claws sharper than needles.
My eyes colder than stone.

Fire roars out of my mouth,
Fierce tongues of flame
Seek out my enemy.

My tail will lash you to pieces
My jaws will grind you to dust
I am the dragon of the bedroom.

No you're not Samantha
I am the dragon in the house
Get your bedroom tidy - or else.

Charlene Corrigan (9) Crown Wood School

THE WAR

The wind blows hard across the empty street
Blowing paper bags about,
Making a rustling sound over the silent roads.

Then the siren goes.
A low wailing sound,
Getting louder and more terrifying by the second.

Now the street is a hive of activity,
Frightened people rushing about,
Like ants, looking for shelter before the bombs drop.

The bombs are screaming down,
All without mercy,
Leaving behind a scene of devastation.

And they're gone.
The people come out of hiding,
And go about collecting their remaining possessions.

Trying to rebuild their shattered lives
Until the next attack occurs.

Hannah Chapman (11) Claycots Middle School

THE GREAT TORNADO

The swirling and twirling tornado is whirling.
Lashing its thundering claws.
It is thumping like a hammer as it goes.
It is tearing things apart.
This time the tornado has a flash as bright as a rainbow
Swaying with all bright lights.
Now the tornado has gone for ever and ever.
The world is destroyed.
Nothing is left but a mess in its path.

Anthony Proctor (10) Claycots Middle School

WORLD WAR II

Dark, deserted and soundless,
The sky is dull with clouds.
Still nothing to be seen
Until a whole squadron of German planes
Come gliding over the small town
Cruising through the air like eagles.
Drifting above, dropping bombs
Without a care.
Then all of a sudden. Crash!
The sound of people crying and screaming
The sound of ambulances ringing
The sound of *death!*

Victor Charles (11) Claycots Middle School

THE WAR

I walk cautiously around the isolated and mournful town,
Nowhere to run, left, right, up or down.
I look down at the blood-covered people,
I stare up at the sky, up at the long church steeple.
Suddenly, I hear screams and a long continuous cry,
The time has come - for me to die.
With a limp in my leg and a bandaged arm,
I run hastily from death, staying hopeful and calm.
I hear bombs and bullets, cries and screams.
I think I'm going forever - that's how it seems.
I see shattered houses and I run faster still,
And then I stop, at my own will.
I find death cowering above my head,
I fall helplessly to the ground,
That's it.
I am dead.

Sheetal Sharma (11) Claycots Middle School

AMBER MY HAMSTER

My hamster Amber is very, very, sweet,
I often come home from school and give her
a little treat,
Her little black eyes come peering up to me,
And I know what she's wondering,
She thinks it's time for tea,
I put her food in her little bowl,
She runs over to it with her little soul,
The night draws in and it becomes very cold,
She runs over to the bars like she's being told,
She climbs up the bars making lots of noise
It sounds like she's crashing all my toys.
I fall asleep eventually,
The morning comes around,
Amber is not making a sound,
Because she is asleep,
Knowing when she wakes up it will be
time to eat,
Amber is one of a kind
A hamster so cute, is so hard to find.

Alison Corney (11) Fox Hill School

SUMMER

Summer is my best season
I like the sun in my hair
There is nothing to compare
With running on the sand
Or over pebbles and the sea
To know how much it feels to be
Free.
This is the season for me.

Vicky Novelle (11) Fox Hill School

DREAM PONY

We galloped away my unicorn and me,
Over the mountains and through the sea,
We dodged through the trees and splashed in the waves,
We kicked up the sand and entered the caves.
We had a great time, my beauty and I,
The stars were now shining in the dawnlit sky.
Sadly the day had now come to an end,
No more exciting times with my pony to spend.
I must get home quickly, before it's too late,
Mum will be waiting at the garden gate.
I hear a loud noise like a telephone ringing,
I open my eyes and the birds are all singing.
I jump out of bed, was it really a dream,
I look out the window and see the sunbeam,
Another day is here to start,
But my beautiful unicorn is still in my heart.

Maria Filby (11) Fox Hill School

IN THE SEA

Wet swimming cossy
Water in your ear
Crabs on your toes
Sand in your beer

Swimming in the sea
With your purple rubber ring
Swim right under water
And hear the mermaids sing.

I enjoyed the swim
Didn't mind the beer
Didn't like the crab
But I can't wait till next year.

Laura Fallon (11) Great Hollands Junior School

BORED

I'm bored very bored
I can't think what to do
I yawn and yawn again
I take an exciting trip to the loo.

My brother has started crying
He's being a great big pain
But I'm still as bored as
I bang my head against the window pane.

I wish I knew what to do
I'm as bored as can be
At home life is so boring
If only my parents could see.

My brother's kissing all my toes
He's being a silly sausage
I'm getting really bored now
My brother's taken a hostage
     Me!

I'm bored very bored
I can't think what to do
I yawn and yawn again
What shall I do?

Hannah Findlay (11) Great Hollands Junior School

A PYTHON

A python can open his jaws
As wide as five double doors
The python puts a rabbit inside
Now the poor rabbit has finally died

Matthew Bettison (11) Great Hollands Junior School

MUM AND DAD

My dad is so boring all he does is
Snore,
He never lets me do anything I wish he wasn't
                                        such a bore.

I tell my mum and all she does is stare,
trying to think what to wear.

When my dad stops snoring and that is hardly ever,
All he says is never never never.

When mum stops staring and I really wish she would,

If only they were normal
that would be good.

Lindsay Nash (11) Great Hollands Junior School

THE BEE

The red rose blooming,
In the golden sunlight,
Along came a bee
Attracted to the sight,
Picking up the pollen,
Fly away little bee,
Buzz away
And leave me in peace.

Heidi Clay (11) Great Hollands Junior School

PIANO DREAMS

I gazed at the piano one day
Oh how I wished that I could play
I ran my fingers over the keys
Thinking of musical memories
With just one finger I picked out a tune
My hopes were soaring over the moon
But at last I'm very sorry to say
No one was listening and my cat ran away.

Aimee Dale (10) Great Hollands Junior School

WHAT AM I

My first is in juice but not in drink.
My second is in sun but not in rain.
My third is in north but not in south.
My fourth is in mug but not n cup.
My fifth is in look but not in book.
My sixth is in pen but not in ink
      What am I?

Jamie Hobden (10) Great Hollands Junior School

CHARGE OF THE KNIGHTS

Patiently waiting,
Tension inflating.
Enemy in sight,
Gather all your might.
Lance in rest,
Dragon crest.
Fast from slow,
Here we go.
Galloping on,
Arm strong.
Enemy encountered,
On foot or mounted.
Swords clashing,
Arrows flashing.
Weapon on shield,
Who will yield?
Helmet is struck,
Deflected, what luck.
Armour has a dent,
Metal bent.
Blood and gore,
More and more.
Clatter of feet,
Enemy retreat.
Victory cry!
But many lie,
Where they die.

Joel Baker (11) Great Hollands Junior School

THE HOLE

I stare at the hole
Gaping wide,
All black and dark inside.
Deep and never ending.
I'm afraid.
I wonder how it was made,
I look down.
The soil is a murky brown
There is no noise from the hole
Could it have been made by a giant mole?

I drop a stone
Not hearing it land,
And there I stand,
Not feeling very grand.
The howling wind
Echoes in the cavern,
Could it be heaven?
The leaves flutter down
And down.
I look once more,
Or could it lead to the Earth's core.

But I feel no heat,
And wonder what the hole would meet.
I leave the hole.
Still gaping wide,
Many mysteries are still inside.

Christopher Tarry (11) Great Hollands Junior School

BARRY'S RABBIT

Barry's rabbit,
Has a very bad habit,
It picks its nose,
Then chews the hose.
It plays with the mouse,
Takes it in the house,
It chews the door,
And chews some more!
It's in a bad mood,
When it wants some food,
When he puts it in a cage,
It has an outrage!
It chews open tins,
And throws them in the bin,
Yes Barry's rabbit,
Has a very bad habit,
If I were Barry,
I'd give it to Harry,
Let him suffer,
I won't have to bother.

Daniel Brown (10) Harmans Water Junior School

ME AND MY GRANNY

I'm going to see my granny soon,
I really just can't wait,
She gives me sweets, buys me nice new clothes,
And bakes me lots of cakes.

She gives me lots of money,
To buy myself new things,
She even listens to me,
When practising to sing.

She buys me lots of china dolls,
To add to my collection,
And when it comes to Christmas time,
She buys me a selection.

I'm going to see my granny soon,
I really just can't wait,
She gives me sweets, buys me nice new clothes,
And bakes me lots of cakes.

Jenny Grace (11) Harmans Water Junior School

MY FRIEND THE MONSTER

I have a friend who is a monster,
who sleeps under my bed at night,
He gets me up in the morning with a tickle and a smile so bright,
I love my friend the monster,
He's the best friend I ever had,
We play games and never stop laughing,
but sometimes he makes me so mad,
He's such a naughty monster sometimes,
but it doesn't matter to me,
because I love my friend the monster,
and he loves me.

Elizabeth Clark (9) Harmans Water Junior School

THE WITCH

Once upon a time there was a haunted house.
The lady who lives in it had a little mouse.
The lady was a witch,
Her wrinkles used to itch,
She was very good at spells,
And a very good nose for smells.
One day the little mouse ran out,
The witch, she chased it all about.
The witch, she cast a horrible spell,
And put the mouse down a deep, dark well.
The mouse was never seen again,
And the witch flew of down the lane.

Matthew Burnett (8) Harmans Water Junior School

POPPIES

Across the open fields,
Perfect in every way,
Pretty as a picture,
Oh it takes your breath away,
You and I can go and see,
Now you know how beautiful they can be;
Some are red some are yellow and some can be white,
how many colours are there?
I guess I'll never know;

Oh in that field where poppies grow.

Charlotte Thatcher (11) Hungerford CP School

A POEM ABOUT CHRISTMAS

Presents under the Christmas tree
The whole house filled with Christmas glee.

No more swimming no more sun,
A super soaker's out of the holiday fun.

A card to uncle Herbert, a card to uncle Harold,
Oh I hate sending Christmas cards let's sing some carols!

Now Christmas is over no more nice or hearty,
Oh I hate all this grumpiness,
Let's go have a New Year's party.

Josh Finesilver (10) Hungerford CP School

THE YELLOW CARAVAN

T he yellow caravan is as old as can be
H awthorn twirls around the chimney
E ggs from crows lie on the sofa

Y ellow is not to be seen rust is covering it
E vening comes and all is still
L ambs graze nearby
L ight flows in to the window as morning breaks
O n the step lies a sleeping cat
W ater leaks from the roof

C at lies in the early morning sun
A nd the mice hide in the old bin
R oses grow near the open window
A n ivy bush brushes against the side
V iolets grow in a clump near the wheel
A nd a rabbit hides in the open cupboard
N ow the caravan is quiet again.

Laura Horne (10) Hungerford CP School

SUMMER ON THE BEACH

S ilky sand gliding through my feet
U nlike the dirt at home
M iddle of summer is the time for me
M idnight magic by the sea
E verything I see is
R emembered by me

O n the sandy beach
N othing could be as wonderful as that

T he town full of people
H appy as can be
E verybody saying hello

B ecause everybody likes one another
E verybody in the sea
A seagull takes my sandwich
C atching it well at least trying
H ome again.

Emma Hunter (11) Hungerford CP School

BILLY JOE

There was a little kitten
His name was Billy Joe
He sat upon the window sill
Watching falling snow

He's really really sweet
The others think him neat
As he sits upon the window sill
Licking his little feet

What's that long white thing
It isn't snow
Can I reach it
I don't know

It would be nice to have a go
Swinging here swinging there
To and fro
Here I go.

Rebecca Moore (10) Lynch Hill Combined School

MY DOG

My dog is black and white
His eyes are not quite right
One is green and one is brown
My mum says he should be put down

My dog is not young he is old
He does not like being out in the cold
He sleeps beside my bed at night
To make sure everything is alright

I take him for walks twice a day
All the cats run away
The birds fly up into the sky
My dog gives out a big sigh

I love my dog with all my heart
I hope we never have to part
I know one day he will die
And that will be the day I cry.

Lisa Fraser (11) Lynch Hill Combined School

WHICH WITCH?

Ms Trim had a twin sister
Who was as ugly as a blister
It could really make you twitch
Trying to tell you which witch is which

Mrs Snichnose is her name
Her and Trim look the same
It could give you a stitch
Trying to guess which witch is which

They both have a pointed nose
One hundred teeth and thirty toes
It can really make you itch
Guessing which witch is which

They live in the sewer
And sleep in cows' manure
You could really get very rich
Taking bets on which witch is which

But there's one thing you can do
Next time you see the two
Anthony Mathews is all you say
And Ms Trim will run away.

Anthony Mathews (10) Lynch Hill Combined School

TEACHERS

Some are old
and some are young,
some are boring
and some are fun.

Some are big
and some are small.
but most are really
boring talking in the hall.

Ms Trim
is really dim.

Mrs Ingham
looks like Spam.

Mrs Lovell,
should be picked up by a shovel.

Mrs May,
is boring every day.

Mrs Steinhardt,
is not smart.

Mrs Coffey,
rots her teeth with toffee.

Some are thin
and some are fat,
but most are as lazy
as a smelly old cat.

Damien Woodall (11) Lynch Hill Combined School

HOLLY

Holly is a chestnut mare
Who is a little Welsh pony
Who has really beautiful hair
But once she was really bony
But now she is very fit.

She was shut in a stable
Covered in dirt, but still forced to carry a rider
Although she wasn't able
Only sharing her stable with a spider.

But now she is always happy
At her new home, with her best friend Pepsi
She's getting rather old
But still is fit and still very bold.

Everyone says she's old and will die
I believe
That at the grand old age of 28
I think she'll survive.

But one day, I went to see her
But she didn't answer to her name
I went to her owner and asked
She took me somewhere
To a garden and there it said
      In loving memory of
         Holly
With flowers round it.

Joanna Hussey (11) Lynch Hill Combined School

THE WOODS

If you go down to the woods today
You're in for a big surprise
If you go down to the woods today
You'd better cover your eyes
'Cause mum and dad
Are really mad
And aunty Rose
Is picking her nose
And aunty Flo
Is having a go at Grandad.

If you go down to the woods today
You're in for a real surprise
If you go down to the woods today
You'd better cover your eyes
'Cause bro and sis
Keep hissing at Miss
And uncle Tim
Is being dim
And aunty Flo's
Still having a go at Grandad.

Hayley Lightfoot (11) Lynch Hill Combined School

WEATHER

Stormy clouds on a windy day,
Approaching rain dropping on its way.
Big puddles turn into streams,
Shiny droplets start to gleam.

A crash of thunder, a thrilling sight
All the birds tucked up tight.
Clouds break away, the sun is free,
The woodpecker comes out of the old oak tree.

A tulip opens to welcome the sun.
The spring has a gust of playful fun.
Warmness and comfy as snug as a bug,
Out comes the snails, the mole and a slug.

Colours beam across the skies,
A rainbow forming until it dies.
White clouds press together,
We've got to go out whatever the weather.

Cold patterns drifting down,
Ants and woodlice begin to drown.
A sheet of snow covers the garden,
Bits of grass begin to harden.

Icicles glisten from the ledges,
Bits of frost stuck to hedges.
Every gutter collects some snow,
All the flowers droop down low.

Then the snow clears away,
Stormy clouds on a windy day . . .

John Briggs (10) Nine Mile Ride CP School

CLOUDS

Imagine living in the clouds
How wonderful it would be
High above the birds.
I could go wherever I want!

Planes would see me fly by
Then suddenly, black smoke
                comes floating up.
What is it?
No! It can't be.

The air is dark
And the clouds have faded
Is it the end of my dream?

Toni D'Amaro (11) Our Lady of Peace Middle School

SUMMER'S DAY

Sitting on the lawn,
Watching time fly by,
Fluffy, puffy, clouds,
Spreading across the sky.
Yellow country meadows,
Pollen in the breeze,
Nature! Nature! Nature!
Boy! What a sneeze.

The day is upside-down,
The sun is beating the ground,
Thirsting for some water,
Clouds building up,
Crowding out the sun.
Then some droplets from the sky,
Now the rain is near.

Peter Donnelly (11) Our Lady of Peace Middle School

A RAIN FOREST

Peace in the rain forest
Silence all around
No man-kind nearby
All creatures safe and sound
No noise from chainsaws
Or other big machines
Just the sound of humming
    coming from the trees
The sun starts to fade away
It wasn't here to stay
So down comes the rain
The creatures are relieved
    that water is here
Now they know they are safe

So now the rain has gone
The creatures run and run
For they know the workmen
    have come
They hear the big machines
    coming from afar
The men jump out of their trucks
Holding chainsaws in their arms
Thousands of creatures' homes
    being destroyed
Day by day
What can we do to make them
    go away?

Christopher Loudon (10) Our Lady of Peace Middle School

SEAWORLD

All the creatures swirling about,
Every child has a smile
Even if for a little while,
Great big whales diving in and out
      of the water
Getting everyone wet.

Whales performing tricks,
Trainers standing on the whales holding
      onto their fins,
Watch them eat all the tiny little fish
As they go down, down and down,

They are full of energy
Look at their shiny skin
Shining in the sunlight,
Lovely and bright
How I wish I could stroke it.

Kirsty Akehurst (11) Our Lady of Peace Middle School

FORGIVENESS

When we forgive we should mean what we say.
We all know how hard it is just to say sorry.
But when we ask God for forgiveness he will always give
you forgiveness.
God is the creator,
He created man to make sure that man did not fight but
Loved and forgave each other.

Roshni Vadher (11) Our Lady of Peace Middle School

MY BEST FRIEND

Natasha's my best friend
I like her a lot
Sometimes she's clever
And sometimes she's not

She's short and chubby
but I don't care
As long as she's my friend
And she's always there

She is very funny
With jokes she tells
Sometimes they're boring
Sometimes they're swell.

Lorraine McGuckian (11) Our Lady of Peace Middle School

A SHARK

A shark is like a torpedo
Shooting through the water,
A shark is the king of the sea
Smashing through the waves,
A shark is like a wild cat
Prowling the sea bed,
A shark is like a butcher
Ripping its meat apart,
A shark is like a hunter
Killing its prey in one blow,
A shark is like a sports car
Speeding along the water,
A shark is like a submarine
Gliding through the ocean,
A shark is like a swan
Swimming so exquisitely

Aaron Bond (11) Our Lady of Peace Middle School

KATE

When I was in nursery
    I met a girl called Kate
We used to have so much fun
But now I have moved away
    from the games we played in the sun.

As we grew older,
    we became more and more mature.
I grew more successful.
    so did Kate
You can be sure!

Kate was always top of the class
    and I was slightly lower
But then I grew higher
    and higher
Then I was just by her.

As we finished year five,
    I left the school and Kate
I wanted to go back
    and see her
But it was just too late!

But now I sleep at her house
And she sleeps at mine
All the good times
    have come back
Just like cherry wine.

On school days I miss her
It is very hard to be happy,
    especially without Kate
I miss all the fun,
    I had with my best mate!

Denise Morris (11) Our Lady of Peace Middle School

ON A HOT SUMMER DAY

On a hot summer day,
I always like to play,
The weather is warm,
On a summer morn,

On a hot summer day,
I always like to play,
I ride my bike,
And give people a fright,

On a hot summer day,
I always like to play,
With my little rabbit,
And that's just a habit,

On a hot summer day,
I always like to play,
I listen to my radio,
And the neighbours say 'Oh no!'

On a hot summer day,
I always like to play,
But as the sun disappears,
It brings back some fears.

Raymond Stahacz (11) Our Lady of Peace Middle School

THE FAIRY OF SPRING

The fairy of spring has come again.
She is spreading out her wings to pervade every corner.
Her fingers are affecting every delicate flower.
Her diminutive feet are making the grass
    fluctuate with the mellow breeze.
Now her grace is shared among us be content.

Rebecca Sheldon (11) Our Lady of Peace Middle School

RACISM

Racism is a real pain
Sometimes it drives me insane
What's the problem with a different race?
Why can't the world live in grace?

Why do black and white have to fight?
At the end of the tunnel there's a glimmer of light
Different races fight in the street
Why aren't people kind to everyone they meet?

Why can people be so violent?
From God is us good people he sent
To them their colours are opposite
Maybe they can work it out bit by bit.

Racism is such a pest
To good things it can infest
Why can't someone come up with an idea?
So the good people have nothing to fear.

Oh no! I'm going mad
Seeing fighting people makes me so sad
No I'm talking about a bad insert
I'm talking about people getting hurt.

I sit here looking at the moon
I pray to God the war will stop soon
I hope this isn't world war three
I see people scared up in a tree.

I see people in fear trembling
This racism is an evil thing
God taught us to be kind
But the racism solution I cannot find.

The war had ended, I'm really glad
Now there's no reason to be sad!

Justin Munt (11) Our Lady of Peace Middle School

THE ICE-CREAM

The soft creamy ice-cream
That caves in to the touch
Its crispy casing, the cone
The taste is too dreamy for words
With so many flavours
It's hard to choose one.

There's vanilla the killer
Mint chocolate chip with a toffee dip
There's strawberry of course
       with chocolate sauce
There are many other
Flavours galore, so many
I can not mention them all.

I go down to the shop
They have sweet lolly pops
The ice-cream I want is
       86 pence
If I buy some 14p gum
It will more than likely
       add up the sum.

I stroll out of the shop
In a world of my own
I unwrap my ice-cream
I feel its tingling on my tongue
As I plunge into a whirlpool
Of mouth-watering luscious ice-cream.

Angela Mullix (10) Our Lady of Peace Middle School

THE ROAD TO HEAVEN

I'll be waiting for you
On the road to heaven
It's really not a long way to go
You'll be safe with me
On the road to heaven
It's time I let you know

It's time to come into this new place
Now it's your turn to come with me
Come up high, up high with me
Up into the kingdom where you belong
Now it's your turn to come with me
Come and follow me this is the right way

There's a person waiting for you
In that mighty place
The highest God of all
He is waiting for you to come
In that mighty place
It's now your time to go

Anna Noctor (11) Our Lady of Peace Middle School

DEATH!

Death means nothingness, loneliness
    and fear
We all die sometime and lose our
    near.
Things could happen to us while
    we are dead.
We will be gone forever
Our stories never read

Death comes naturally, never
　with force
Unless with poison, then you let
　it take its course.

Nothing to do, just turn in
　our graves
We could be cremated and
　be set off in flames

Death comes naturally, never
　with force
Unless with poison, then you let
　it take its course

It's hard to take in you might
　die one day
You could be buried and
　fade away

Natasha Reddy (11) Our Lady of Peace Middle School

THE COLDEST DAY

I look out of my window, a winter's day
has fallen over the land.
Animals retreat, back to their homes.
They just want to escape from icy cold air
go outside to see just how cold it really is.
　　　I take one step out, I hear the
crunch of coldness, cold air seeping
into my veins, the tips of my fingers are
getting number and number.
I rush back indoors, into my room and
straight under the blanket.
　　　The coldest day has won another battle
and I was his victim.

Joelle Dupont (11) Our Lady of Peace Middle School

GHOSTS!

G   hosts have been in my house,
       I saw them in the cellar.
       They were drinking my mum's best wine.
       I think I'd better tell her.

H   undreds of happy ghosts,
       Getting drunk from the wine.
       Making fun out of my dolly,
       Hey! That dolly's mine!

O   bese ghosts doing funny things,
       Making funny faces, jokes and dreams.
       I felt like going over to them,
       And asking them if I could join in.

S   ome people say that they are scary,
       But I think that they are quite nice.
       They're better than people made them out to be.
       Three times better! Thrice!

T   hey're said to be spooky, scary, pale things,
       Which are ashen white.
       They are not opaque but transparent,
       They would give you such a fright.

Natasha Ansari (11) Our Lady of Peace Middle School

THE BAND

There once was a band
A very strange group
With lions and tigers
And even a newt.
The lion played the trumpet
The elephant the bassoon,
And the violin was played by the
                silly old baboon.

They played in a concert
In a very big hall
They sold many tickets
But still the crowd was small.
They all played their hearts out
And people had to admit,
This animal band
Were a big hit!

Tony O'Donnell (11) Our Lady of Peace Middle School

THE DOOR THAT'S NEVER BEEN OPENED

What's behind the door I have never dared to open?
Where it leads to no one knows.
Maybe there's a world where no one ever dies
Maybe there's a wonderland with pink and purple skies,
Maybe there's a place with meadows all around,
Maybe there's a sullen world with no happiness or sound.
What's behind the door I have never dared to open?
Where it leads to no one knows.
A sea with glistening seaweed, mermaids and pearls
Deserted moorland which is green as emeralds,
A joyful, happy place with children having fun,
Maybe there's nothing but a deep black hole,
A futuristic place with robots and computers
What's behind the door I have never dared to open?
Where it leads to no one knows.
A place full of dreams and wishes that come true
A heaven perhaps
Or a world full of sorrow, anguish and sadness
What's behind the door I have never dared to open?
Where it leads to no one knows

Amanda Button (11) Our Lady of Peace Middle School

SPRING'S GIFTS

Spring brings lots of gifts to me.
Lots of trees blossoming making the world
a beautiful place to live!
Birds twittering as they build their new nests.
Joyful families in fields playing games
and admiring the newly born carefree animals,
hopping around under the spring sunshine.
Lots more animals are being born into
the world and are coming out of hibernation.
I see people enjoying the beauty of the
spring flowers.
I feel the sun's rays beating down on
my head as I wait for a breath of
the cool spring air.

Katie-Sian Power (11) Our Lady of Peace Middle School

THE WORLD

The world was made for us,
But now we ruin it,
We destroy the rain-forests,
Cut them down,
Destroying the homes of little animals,
Only to build big factories which destroy the
                                   o-zone layer
Why! Why! Are we doing this?

In our neighbourhood,
Punk kids are ruining it, by spraying graffiti
If we do something now we might not be too late,
For the world is being destroyed.

Daniel Almeida (10) Our Lady of Peace Middle School

VICTORY

There was a sudden bang,
I wondered what it meant.
I had heard rumours,
That the Enemy had been sent.

So I went to go and see,
What was going on,
But I accidentally got caught,
They told me He was gone.

Who's he I muttered quietly,
I saw a glimpse of blood on deck,
They said he had been badly hurt,
But someone had gone to check.

I was pushed into a cupboard,
In the confusion that took place.
There was gunpowder in there,
And very little space.

I seemed to doze for ages,
The noise just carried on,
Then the door slid open,
All the daylight had gone.

A bright light appeared.
A casualty was brought down,
Our Captain was coming nearer,
His face set in a frown.

There was quite a conversation,
'We've beaten the Enemy'
The last I heard were Nelson's words,
'My dear friend Hardy, Kiss me'.

Emma-Louise Walton (10) Our Lady of Peace Middle School

THE WEATHER

Sunny, raining, cloudy, snowing
that's the way the weather
is going.
I go out into the garden
wearing a T shirt and it
starts to rain.
I go upstairs to put a
jumper on and the sun
comes out again.
You never know how the
weather will stay, that's
why it's so hard to go out
to play.

Elizabeth Jane Kennedy (10) Our Lady of Peace Middle School

SHOOTING STAR

I stare out the window,
Not knowing where to look,
For all I see is darkness,
No sign of any light.
Then suddenly I see a light,
Although it seems unreal.
What could it be?
This thing I see.
It could be the future,
Or a distant building ablaze,
Or a sign for all people to
gaze,
At the beauty of the night.

Siobhan Taylor (10) Our Lady of Peace Middle School

SPRING

It is dawn once more, in the same place I have come
to love and cherish. But it is neither autumn nor
Winter but it is spring! I hear the same whoosh of
wind and same swoop of birds. But there is a new,
unfamiliar sound, I listen harder: it is the
sound of a gentle hedgehog walking along
the ground, making a tip, tip sound. I see leaves
coming back on the trees. I see the same corn-fields
reflecting the sun's light, and I see the same
pond, no more frozen.
I pick up a flower to smell. I crouch down to
feel the smooth grass. I feel the wind brush
against me.

Kevin Loughlin (10) Our Lady of Peace Middle School

PEACE

Stop this war,
End this crime,
It's gone too far,
now is the time,
Put out the flames,
Produce the dove,
Reject the war,
For peace and love.

Coffins lowered,
Too many die,
child's tears,
Mothers cry,
Surrender and mercy,
Begging and plead,
The war is over,
Let's plant the seed.

Hayley Peters (10) Our Lady of Peace Middle School

SPRING SECRET PLACE

We heard birds' lovely singing.
Some birds sang a beautiful
Song because it was becoming spring,
Oh! Lovely spring! We heard the whistling
wind go past us. The wind was a
very soft wind, it was like a mother
putting her baby to sleep. We saw the sun
rise into the lovely blue sky. The sun was
pure yellow - we know now why it is spring.
It was becoming midday we smelt a sweet
thing - we didn't know what it was. We looked
around and suddenly we saw hundreds of spring
flowers, surrounded by a big spring- green field. Oh!
It was beautiful! There were daffodils, crocuses,
Snowdrops, and all sorts of spring flowers.
The daffodils were lovely, some were
yellow round the outside and orange in the
middle. The crocuses were beautiful too, they
were purple and smelled lovely, like perfume.
The snowdrops were, pure, clean, white, the loveliest
flowers I have ever seen, it was my first time
to see snowdrops. It was becoming dusk.
We saw the beautiful sunset, the colours
were beautiful we saw red, pink, purple, and
blue. It was a lovely and beautiful day.

Paula Kerins (10) Our Lady of Peace Middle School

MY SECRET PLACE

The cold wind is blowing softly among the trees,
the white frost, white as the clouds, lies on the cool
green grass.
The sky is as blue as blue bells on the stem.
The trees as bare as can be, as spring is coming
for new life will appear. The bare trees covered in
a white coat of frost. I smell the fresh air that blows
around and the smell of frost makes me cold.
It starts raining.
The clear diamond water dropping from heaven.
On the trees the water comes down, like on a slide,
then flying for a landing to the soft ground, into the
roots of the trees and plants.

Tarandip Rehal (10) Our Lady of Peace Middle School

BONES

Have you heard of those things called bones?
You know; something everybody owns.
They are inside your arms and your legs,
But are not inside any eggs.
You have to try not to fall
Or it might break your socket and ball.
Try not to fall and hurt your meta-tarsels
or you won't be walking in castles
I'll tell you what surprises me -
It's what you can do with a knee
Without it running away from your body:
I've wondered that since I was three!

Nick Bell (10) Our Lady of Peace Middle School

SPRING

I can hear the birds twittering in the
sky as they fly past me. There
are sounds from little insects in the
ground like bees buzzing from flower
to flower, picking up pollen and
flies flying around in the air.
I can see daffodils in a field
beneath some raspberry bushes
and a bunch of crocuses right
in the middle of the field.
sitting there in the sunshine. It
starts to get a bit breezy as
we stand there by all the
crocuses. I can see a little wild
rabbit hopping across the field
as his little legs start to hop
through the trees, until he has
disappeared, I feel the lumps on the
trees and the soft grass as I go
to pick up a daffodil. It starts
to get colder as it gets to
late midday when all the bees,
flies and birds start to go back
into their nests.

Sean Ryan (10) Our Lady of Peace Middle School

SPRING!

I can feel
        the soft breeze blowing
through my hair. I can feel the soft
lush grass underfoot. I can feel the
warm sun shining on me.

I can see
>   the clear running waters. I can see
the light blue sky in the distance.
I can see flowers opening very slowly.

I can hear
>   the birds singing happily. I can hear
children playing. I can hear wasps buzzing
around.
>   That is what I can
>   feel, see and hear in
>   the spring time.

Nathan Wood (11) Our Lady of Peace Middle School

MY SECRET PLACE: SPRING

I can hear a frog croak, a few birds are
twittering sweet, early morning songs. Water is
tumbling off a cliff.
A tall tree stands strong with fabulous green
leaves, brown bark on the trunk.
Daffodils are pouring on each other with
green stems. A dear is drinking water from a
stream, birds hunting prey for their young ones.
Strong tough logs are cut from benches, rough stones,
bark on the floor. Rabbits are awake happily
bouncing on each other. Squirrels running up and
down the trees, worms crawling up to the surface,
bees and a few wasps flying about each other.
Flowers smelling lovely, apples ripe and juicy, sleepy birds
fly back to their nests, deer galloping to their homes,
worms crawling back under the ground, bees stop
collecting pollen and fly back to their hives to see
dawn in the morning.

Emma Shearer (10) Our Lady of Peace Middle School

PEACE

O' Lord open my eyes
and let me see the world
bring peace to our world
comfort me and comfort
them. When the world is
full of war only you
can stop it.

      Amen

Michael James (10) Our Lady of Peace Middle School

MY SECRET PLACE

In my secret place all I can hear is the wind blowing,
harshly as it stirs the swaying, frozen, crispy grass.
I can hear the snow as it melts and drips off the bare
but beautiful trees.
In the middle of the field there are no cars rushing or zooming
past,
nothing to disturb the wonderful peace.
I can also hear birds tweeting and twittering up high in the
icy, frosty trees, slightly swaying in the cold but gentle wind.
I hear the small, tiny field mice,
scuttling and rustling around in the tall frosty grass.
The tiny, little, hungry birds are flying, quickly around,
in the wonderfully blue sky in search of food.
The blue sky does not even have one fluffy, white cloud in it.
I see a bedraggled, old spider's web,
glistening and twinkling in the morning sun as it shines down
on the wonderful web.

Lauren Godfrey (10) Our Lady of Peace Middle School

RETURN TO THE SECRET PLACE

I can hear the gentle twitter of the little birds.
The mild breeze makes the bright green grass
slowly sway from side to side. Makes the
morning frost crack like a glass being
dropped. The light breeze makes the delicate
flowers softly sway. I can see candy-floss
clouds slowly drift away. The knobbly blown
trees are covered in fluffy pink blossom.
The magnificent yellow daffodils look as if
they are made of soft silk. I can smell
the gorgeous, fresh pollen drifting from
the tiny flowers. I can almost taste the
spring freshness of the luscious spiky
grass.

I can see the fiery orange sun
beating down on the melting morning
frost. The sky is filled with beautifully
coloured birds.

The sky is filled with pink cotton
wool clouds. The sky looks as if it is a crispy
cherry pie that's just been cut in half. The
tired birds go back to their uncomfortable
nests.

Sebastien Butcher (10) Our Lady of Peace Middle School

WINTER VICTIM

My feet crunch and crackle the golden leaves
The birds sing gaily and happily.
The woodpecker taps out a sturdy rhythm.
The shadows lumber out of the bright plants
Like huge treacherous monsters.
I can hear some ducks quack away at some
Frosted weed like owls fighting at their prey.
Trotting of shire horses fade away gently.
The crackling of twigs
Sound like a fire with sparks flying off
The smell of cold
Haunts the grass
Winter is taking place

Niall Brophy (10) Our Lady of Peace Middle School

I LOVE THE SPRING

Spring is such a wonderful thing
It gives us pretty birds that sing.
It gives us blossom, buds and trees
It gives us butterflies and bees.
The fruit and flowers begin to grow
There is no sign of hail or snow.
The sun is shining bright and clear
And makes us happy to be here.
Nature's at its best in spring
Showing us God's wondrous things.

Gina Mundee (10) Our Lady of Peace Middle School

MY SECRET PLACE: SPRING

The dawn's sun welcomes us as it appears
slowly through the cold, bitter mist.
The new baby birds are twittering sweetly,
While their mum gathers worms to feed them.
The animals slowly wake up from their long,
Dreamless days of hibernation.
Hear the wet dew drip to the ground from the new,
Fresh, green leaves on the enormous, bald trees.
The leaves on the big trees are approaching
Thousands by thousand.
See the blue sky with a few fluffy, white clouds
Just like pieces of cotton wool.
The pretty, pink primroses are blooming,
While it approaches midday.
Strong perfumed, new spring, sweet smelling flowers.
Silky, smooth, flower petals.
Rabbits hop from one dark hole to another.
With their fluffy tails all cuddly and white,
Bobbing up and down.
The scented breeze wakes me from my daydream,
As it passes my nose.
Dusk arrives,
As the sun sets beyond the horizon.
The delicious taste of someone's barbecue,
Makes my mouth water.

Claire Griffin (10) Our Lady of Peace Middle School

THE CHEETAH

Prowling up to the gazelle
It runs so gracefully and so fast
Then pounces on its prey
And tears it to pieces with its sharp pointed teeth
What pure hell for the gazelle
The pain, the fright, it's scared to death
As the predator sinks its teeth into its flesh
It died a bloody death
But it was the cheetah's family meal.

Erin Brown (9) Our Lady of Peace Middle School

MUSIC

As it plays its tune,
And sings its song,
The gentle loving music,
Like floating on air.

The melody goes on,
Like winding string,
The song of life,
Brings pictures of time.

As pictures form,
In my mind,
Fun and playing
No cares or foes

As it falls to an end,
It fades away,
The melody slows,
The path takes end.

Fiona Green (11) Our Lady of Peace Middle School

LOSING AIR

I need to get out
This is a dead end room
I'm punching and kicking
but I think it's my doom

I've got to hide
I can't get away
Trapped in a cave
And never seen light of day

Oh no it's here
It's become my last day
Now I've got a real fear
I need to run away

I'm getting trapped under
I want to explode
I need medication
Or maybe a code

Hoping in vain
I want to get out
This pain
It's driving me insane

I need some help
Please come right now
This isn't fair
I'm losing air

I demolished the walls
I can feel the cold air
I can see light of day
Now this is fair.

Richard Swiatek (11) Our Lady of Peace Middle School

SPACE

    Space is a dark, solemn place
A lonely, isolated, scary place
Old and twisted
Space is the place of a billion
    lives
Space has claimed many lives
But still hungry for more
Many people have braved the
    twisted space
Some that went, not to return
Space is an unforgiving place
The place of a billion lives
The old and twisted space.

James Cook (11) Our Lady of Peace Middle School

IN THE DEAD OF THE NIGHT

In the dead of the night,
My eyes alight,
A strange sound came to my ears,
Was it my brother,
Was it my mother
Or was it the worst of my fears,
Wise owls hooting,
Lonely dogs barking,
Cats a courting
A tap carelessly left dripping,
Cooling radiator pipes contracting and groaning?
Then I fell asleep.

Georgia Mann (8) Our Lady of Peace Middle School

THE ROAD THAT LEADS TO NOWHERE

For many years I had wondered what lay beyond that wall,
A wall that hid me from a world full of selfishness and lust,
A wall towering high with gloomy grey bricks,
Concealing the world from me.

The whistling of the wind captured my breath,
Overtaking it with pleasant impressions
Of the sweet smell of nature's fragrance,
And chattering birds perching on the tree tops.

Cracks in the dusty bricks showed me
A stream where roaring dragons raced down,
Leaving clouds of smoke trailing behind.
Beautiful trees and plants growing wild,
A different world of tranquillity and natural beauty.

Being freed from this prisoned world
Would fulfil my hopes and dreams.

As I grew older, this world was no more
Than where I was before.
Its beauty had blinded and deserted all its victims,
Led us to a place where an incomplete jigsaw lay.
Isolation and fear grew inside me.

The wall was my childhood,
My old life, my memories,
But my memories are blank and vague.

Don't make the mistake I made,
For your childhood is like time,
One minute it is there . . .
And the next, it is . . .
Going, going, gone . . .

Jenna Graham (11) Our Lady of Peace Middle School

MY SECRET PLACE

I have a secret place all to myself,
Where alone it's me, and me alone.
I can feel the smooth, silky sand
Crunching beneath my bare feet,
and I can hear the hungry seagulls,
swooping and screeching above me.
I can see, tiny delicate shells,
Sparkling and glistening in the
        blazing sun,
They are just like shining emeralds,
Just washed up by the early wave.

The sea is like a young baby,
Rolling in the sunshine.
The foam on top is like handsome
        white horses,
Racing to the finish-line,
the sandy shore.
It laps against the sand so gently,
        so gently.

I look around my favourite place,
and I know I will never part with it.

Sarah O'Shea (11) Our Lady of Peace Middle School

A FIRE

The fire burns, pops and rumbles
Crunching and snapping.
The fire is hot as a sun.
It is as big as a tree.
The wood turns black
The flames are gone
All you can see is ashes.

Richard Wheeler (9) Our Lady of Peace Middle School

BONES

Bones, bones are happy old bones. They hold me up
and keep me up!
Funny bones, shoulder bones and many many more
play their part on a different floor!
There's the skull floor hip floor and quite a few more.
But at the end of the day
I'd just like to say
I love to relax my trying old bones in a lovely, bubbly
    Hot Bath!

Chris Arthur (9) Our Lady of Peace Middle School

THE STORMY SEA

The stormy sea lies very quiet.
Suddenly the sea starts gliding
The wind starts spinning
the water starts rushing through the air
then the tide forces its way through.
The wind punches, crunches and
munches the sea.
The wind whirls and twirls on
top of the sea.
Slowly they both tinkle down
it is all silent again.

Vibha Vadher (9) Our Lady of Peace Middle School

A FIRE

A hiss, a crackle comes from the fire.
It smells like petrol.
It sounds like a lion's roar.
It's as hot as lava.
It is as high as a tree.
As it gets bigger it gets louder,
and as it gets louder it gets hotter.
It changes everything.
The water puts it out and all that's left
is ashes and a big black patch.

James Carpenter (9) Our Lady of Peace Middle School

MONKEY, MONKEY

Monkey, monkey
climb so high,
reaching out to touch the sky
Swinging, swinging from tree to tree
looking, looking so gracefully,
I hope we will always see,
The swinging monkeys on the trees.
It's down to us the little ones
to make sure the monkey lives.

Clare McLaughlin (9) Our Lady of Peace Middle School

THE WIND

The wicked whirling wind
Breaks through the barriers of the street
Darting and diving
Pushing and pursuing
It taps on the cold door steps
Flying and flapping
It grips everything in its path
Unravelling and destroying
Suddenly the morning sun comes out
Then it blows gently away.

Bharan Kumar (9) Our Lady of Peace Middle School

SOUND OF THE NIGHT

When I lay down
In the night
I sometimes get a
Bit of a fright
I hear the wind whistle
Past my window
I sometimes hear
The leaves fly and flow
sometimes high,
sometimes low,
I hear things creak
up in the loft
I do not speak
I stay as still as a rock

Michael McCormack (9) Our Lady of Peace Middle School

THE RUN AWAY TRAIN

Faster and faster
goes the train
Over the hills
and down the
lane.

Slowing down
the train will stop
under the bridge
and round the block.

Rhia Daniell (9) Our Lady of Peace Middle School

THE TORNADO

Whirling and whizzing
Pulling down houses and throwing them
Destroying as it passes
Knocking down buildings kicking down houses
Cracking windows destroying homes
Violently destroying the city
And very slowly calms down to a breeze.

Ashley James (9) Our Lady of Peace Middle School

AUTUMN

Walking on the crispy leaves
Through the tall bare trees
Crunch!
Go the leaves.
Watch them run across the street
And play chase across the ground.

Becky Campion (9) Our Lady of Peace Middle School

AUTUMN

There's one leaf left
There it hangs on a tree
A knight on horse-back
That's what I see!
The leaf fights to win life
A wind blows
The leaf wounded
Flies like the wings of a dove
Its life is lost
The leaf has fallen

Chloé Thornton (9) Our Lady of Peace Middle School

PEACE!

Peace, peace,
Peace is the word,
God sent peace,
So that we all heard,
No more wars,
No more fight,
Think about the poor,
It's giving them a fright.

Bombs, battle, fight, war!
Stop the killing,
No more,
Come on, pray,
Pray to all
We have to ask,
Until we fall.

Bina Thakrar (9) Our Lady of Peace Middle School

AUTUMN

Leaves are falling
Swirling, twirling
Burnt amber red and beige
Blowing gently across the ground
Crunch crack crumble
The leaves go
The branches became all bare and lonely.

Hannah Webb (9) Our Lady of Peace Middle School

MY SECRET PLACE IN SPRING

The sounds are lovely! You can hear the
Birds twittering and flapping their wings like
someone trying to start up an engine.
The smell is gorgeous, you can smell the
scent of the flowers, rising wakening to start
a new sunny day. The grass is shooting
up from the ground like a volcano erupting.
In my secret place it's like paradise, so if
your hand was dull touch a flower from my
secret place and your whole body will be bright.
At my secret place the sight is wonderful,
You can see the flowers growing and the
animals doing what they usually do. In my
secret place there is a pond and in that pond
there are some fishes playing like happy
little friends. The horrible thing is my secret
place are the bees *ouch* a bee has just
stung me! The unpleasant thing in my secret
place are the bugs as they bite. You get a
great view of the trees and the leaves rising
from their branches.

Luke Davies (10) Our Lady of Peace Middle School

THE WHIRLWIND

It gushed and galloped around the dark streets.
Whirling and enchanting the seas.
Disobeying and maliciously destroying the calmness
Now it has died down.

Louise O'Reily (9) Our Lady of Peace Middle School

THE FLOOD

It tackles the wind
and forces the chairs
Smashes up furniture
and races downstairs.
It twirls and marches
When it goes downstairs
and races to other houses in the air

Andrew Seymour (9) Our Lady of Peace Middle School

BONES

As you can see
The knee is free
To help you move around,
But what is odd,
The bones in your head
Don't go all the way around
The strange thing is
The arms go round
Without falling off on the
Ground!

John Millican (10) Our Lady of Peace Middle School

BONES!

Bones, bones are mad
In your body
Looping this way
and that,
And they
never stop
for a chat.
If your arms
drop down
like an ape,
We're gonna
pick 'em up
And stick you with tape!

Michelle Cox (10) Our Lady of Peace Middle School

MY HOMEWORK IS LATE BECAUSE...

My homework is late because...

My house was on fire
I had to baby sit
I went to Brownies
My library books were over due
I went to a party
We went shopping
My book exploded
There was a good film on TV
My pet alligator was ill
My friends wouldn't stop calling for me
A goblin kidnapped me...

I couldn't be bothered

Charlotte Henderson (10) Parsons Down Junior School

I AM LATE BECAUSE . . .

       I am late because . . .

My car ran out of petrol,
My brother wouldn't get up,
We got stuck in a huge traffic jam
and the door got stuck.

       I am late because . . .
I couldn't find my school bag,
The baby was crying in her cot,
My mum needed some money but my
dad had took the lot.

       I am late because . . .

I forgot it was school today,
So I went out to play.
I went round my friends house,
and never went out all day.

       I am late because . . .

The house caved in on us,
so I couldn't escape of course,

       That's why I'm late, miss.

Michelle Mason (10) Parsons Down Junior School

I AM LATE BECAUSE...

I am late because
My car broke down
My bike had a puncture
I got attacked by bandits
I could not find my tie
My alarm clock did not go off
I had to buy some more milk for my breakfast
I could not find my homework book
I got half-way to school and I did not have my pen
I could not find my glasses
I got stuck in a traffic jam
A Tyrannosaurus Rex stamped on me
My house got blown up
The army decided to attack me
I had to fight the Minotaur
I fell down the stairs
I lost my games kit
I could not find my shoes
King Kong was on the lose
My baby brother threw up and I had to clean it up
I lost my watch
I thought it was a day off
I had to get some rock off the moon
I tried to find my pet ant
I found out my python had eaten it
Aliens zapped me

And that's why I am late!

Luke Dixon (10) Parsons Down Junior School

I AM LATE BECAUSE

I am late because
I missed the bus
The car broke down
I slept in late
The alarm didn't go off
My house was burgled
My house fell down
My mother fainted
The car tyre burst
Our house was flooded right to the top
Our house was on fire
I went to the opticians
It was raining
It was snowing
My bunk bed fell down
My glasses broke
A spider came into the house and my mum got scared
I thought it was a day off
I lost my school uniform
I had to baby-sit
I was chased by a monkey
I lost my tie
My garage blew up into smithereens
My auntie came over on a visit
My homework disappeared into thin air
Our chimney fell off
My eyes dropped out
A plane crashed on our house
My grandad had a heart attack
My cousin was born at one o'clock
My leg dropped off in the car and that's why I was late!

Scott Newport (10) Parsons Down Junior School

MY HOMEWORK IS NOT DONE BECAUSE...

I didn't have time...
We had to go out...
I didn't know what to do...
I knew it would be wrong so I threw
it in the bin...
My pen ran out...
I had to feed my pet elephant...
I thought it was due next Monday...
I really wanted to watch TV...
I had to go to Guides...
I was getting enrolled...
I thought it was Wednesday but it
wasn't it was Friday...
My mum died...
My dad died...
My hamster chewed it up and died of
paper poisoning so I went to his
funeral...
It was my 11th birthday this Monday...

Well really Miss

I could not be bothered to do it.

Catherine Holland (10) Parsons Down Junior School

I AM LATE BECAUSE...

My car broke down,
My brother got up late,
My sister was sick,

I am late because...

My mum was washing up,
My dad came home drunk,
I forgot my pen and had to go back for it,

I am late because . . .

My horse started to fly
My ruler grew and grew
An unknown puppy thought I was dinner and it
ended up in a dogpital,

I am late because . . .

My brother turned into a scorpion and pinched my toe,
My dad turned into a snake and poisoned me,
My mum turned into a panda and put me in the street,
My sister turned into a pony and kicked me over,
and I flew so high I got stuck on a cloud and met God
Oh what a life.

Nikki Arnold (10) Parsons Down Junior School

MY HOMEWORK IS LATE . . .

My homework is late because . . .
My little sister ate it,
My big brother tore it,
My brother and I had to fight,
We had to go out every night,
I could not find my book,
And no-one would help me look,
I lost my pen, my cartridge ran out,
My sister started to mess about,
I had to go to my nan's house,
I had to go to my Gran's house,
I couldn't remember what to do,
The house fell down and buried it,
There was a fire and it burnt my homework,
My mum chucked it in the bin,
My dad used it to blow his nose on,
My sist . . . you don't believe me do you?

Karen Swanborough (10) Parsons Down Junior School

MY HOMEWORK'S LATE BECAUSE . . .

My dog run out of things to chew so he
had a little meal with my homework.
I lost it
I haven't started it yet.
Um,a,uh,uh because um, I don't really know.
Someone stole my homework last night.
I forgot it again.
We were too busy.
It didn't want to go to school today.
My teddy bear took my homework on a trip on
Sunday and hasn't come back yet.
It's at home,
It's found its way to some second-hand kitty
litter.
It's in my old school bag.
I left it at home.
I left it at my grans.
I didn't know we had any in the first place.
We were in a rush and I forgot it.
My sister squashed a spider in my homework and
the spider crawled off with it.
I accidentally buried it with my dead budgie.
My dad became Prime Minister so we were
celebrating all week.
My baby brother was sick on it.

David Caswell (10) Parsons Down Junior School

I WAS LATE BECAUSE

I was late because
My car broke down
I got knocked over by a car
My mum took half an hour on the loo
I was playing football
My alarm clock got smashed to bits
My shirt was dirty
I couldn't find my reading record card
My cat was trying to eat me
My wig was still on the line
I couldn't find my key
When I won the National Lottery I fainted
Medusa haunted me
My cat was sick on me
My tie had a hole in it
I lost four buttons off my shirt
I had to go to the dentist
My pen nib snapped
When I woke up I was burgled
And that is why I am late

Neil Edlin (10) Parsons Down Junior School

I'M LATE BECAUSE

I'm late because . . .

I went to bed too late last night.
My bike had a flat tyre.
My clothes were dirty.
The clock was wrong
My mum cut her finger.
Dad burnt the toast.
The zip on my bag broke.
My mum was on the phone for an hour.
A fish in the pond died.
The sink was blocked.
The cat hurt its paw.
I fell in the pond.
The garage was jammed.
My arm fell off.

So that's why I am late!

Jaimie Davies (10) Parsons Down Junior School

I AM LATE BECAUSE . . .

My Land Rover blew up,
My sister got flushed down the loo,
I couldn't find my under wear,
My baby brother ripped up my reading book,
I stapled my finger,
My football had a hole in it,
The dog shredded my shoes,
The shed fell down,
My big sister fainted,
My ambulance came,
My dad used my reading card to test his blow lamp on,
The taps didn't work,
We had to jump into the pond instead,
My sister tried to pierce my ears,
We had a power cut,
The ceiling fell in,
The cat fell off the roof into the pond,
The kittens copied and jumped off the fence onto the flower bed,
My mum's best plant decided to die,
The dog bolted,
My baby brother disturbed the ant's nest,
The book shelf fell on the rabbit,
The house collapsed,
We got a caravan,
The shower didn't work,
The north wind blew,
The money blew away,
My ruler snapped,
The river flooded the caravan,
We had a street party,
It looks like I got up on the wrong side of life this morning!

Dominic Howard (10) Parsons Down Junior School

MY HOMEWORK IS LATE BECAUSE . . .

My homework is late because . . .
I forgot I had homework to do.
Burglars stole my homework book.
All the pages fell out and I lost them.
My mum put her coffee on it and it spilt.
My dad thought it was rubbish and he threw it out.
I found it again but my brother found it as well
and he was sick and he dribbled on it.
I couldn't think because my sister was singing on
the karaoke.
My dog ran away and I stayed up real late to
find him.
My grandma had a heart attack and we had to take her
to hospital.
I had to go and watch my uncle launch the first
Fairy Liquid bottle into space.
Family crisis, dad forgot it was their anniversary.
My older sister won 100 quid on the Lottery.
We went to Hawaii last night.
A shark ate my grandpa!
So that is why my homework book
is late!

But why am I late? I am afraid
that is another story!

Melissa Banbury (10) Parsons Down Junior School

MY HOMEWORK IS LATE BECAUSE

I dropped it on the way to school.
A van ran over it.
My mum thought it was a newspaper and gave
it to the dog.
I lost it.
My pen ran out.
I went to a castle and lost it in a hole.
It got lost on the beach.
It got stuck up in the tree.
My dad was in hospital.
A hare took it.
It went up the hoover.
It got chopped up with the potatoes.
A space craft came and took it.
It vanished into the air.
A spitfire shot it to pieces.

Sam Bishop (10) Parsons Down Junior School

MY HOMEWORK IS LATE

My homework is late because
My mum thought it was rubbish
My pet bird was not letting me
concentrate
I left it in Alexandria
My mum put wedding photos in it
My rabbit died on it
My dad pinned it to wood
The time went back
My uncle thought it was part of
a motorbike
My brother used it for reading
My best friend stole it
I fell down the sink
My dad's car ran over it
I left it on the table
My sister made paper dolls out of it
I just forgot it.

That's why my homework's late.

Shauna Saunders (9) Parsons Down Junior School

FUN AT THE CIRCUS

At the circus I play games,
fun games sad games silly and spooky games
I scream my loudest

We win prizes teddy bears and things
But cruelty to circus animals means
pleasure for the circus crowd.

Jennifer Bristow (9) Ranikhet Primary School

FLOWER FLOWER

flower flower
grow very tall
some people say
that you're very small

flower flower
you're very bright
flower flower
I know I am
bright.
My petals are
yellow
and my leaves
are green
it's time for a
nap
good night.

Kristina Bray (9) Ranikhet Primary School

ICE-CREAM

I like ice-cream
It tastes nice
It tastes nice when the sun shines out
When it's hot it all melts away
And drip drop drips away on the floor.

When it melts,
Ants and birds come along,
They eat it all up,
I scream real loud in my dad's face,
because I've dropped my poor ice-cream,

Hayley Walker (8) Ranikhet Primary School

THE LITTLE MOUSE

I saw a little mouse he was sitting in
His house. I went to the fridge
To get the cheese because it sat there
And it froze. Then I got a small bowl
I filled it up.
I bathed the mouse then I put him
Back in his house.
He sat there for hours then he went to
Sleep. In the morning it sold himself
Very cheap.

Someone bought him she was
very kind to me
Then she gave me my favourite tea.

Kirsty Bradfield (9) Ranikhet Primary School

RUN RABBIT RUN

A rabbit with no family
All snug in a corner
Has nothing to eat or nothing to drink
But the drip drip drop of the rain.

Suddenly he spots a fox
So quickly up jumped he
Poor rabbit didn't have any choice
but to let fox eat him.

A few days later people knew he passed away,
So no more rabbits went out anymore.

Kailey Bennellick (9) Ranikhet Primary School

CREATURES OF THE WORLD

Fish swim, swimming
Swimming across the sea.

Birds fly, flying
With colours just for me.

Cats meow, meowing
They've got kippers for their tea.

Dogs bow, wowing
bow wow and how do you?

Luke Grover (9) Ranikhet Primary School

THE FLOWER

My master waters me every day,
I am a beautiful flower.
Every day the sun will shine,
Sometimes it rains
But I don't mind,
I am a beautiful flower
I need to get some sleep,
Goodnight everybody,
I will not make a peep

Kylé Holland (9) Ranikhet Primary School

THE DYING PLANET

I left earth
to find another planet
Through space I go
I see a planet ahead
Laser guns I hear
I go and check it out
Space ships moving about
It was a different planet
Altogether there was war
And the planet was destroyed
People dying people fighting
I ask a man
Who is fighting for his life
What is happening
People are appearing out of nowhere

Natalie Jackson (11) Sandy Lane Junior School

THE WIND

The wind is nippy
The wind is nice
The wind can blow
you over twice
The wind makes me
shiver all night.
The wind cools me
down after a sunny
day.
The wind moves the curtain
and howls.
The wind knocks
on the door all night.

Stuart Graham (8) Sandy Lane Junior School

FOOTBALL

Football is cool.
The ball is round and small.
I play football everyday.
And this is what I say.
Football is the best.

Philip James Munday (9) Sandy Lane Junior School

COMPUTER GAMES RAP

Computer games are really cool
Boom ch boom boom ch
I keep on playing virtual pool
Boom ch boom boom ch

Every night I'm in my room
Shooting demons out of doom
Boom ch boom boom ch

Michael Sheldon (8) Sandy Lane Junior School

SIDE BY SIDE IN THE WIND

The breeze blowing
The trees swaying
Side by side in the wind
Branches swaying
Children playing
Side by side in the wind
Leaves falling to the ground
Side by side in the wind

Rhea Carter (9) Sandy Lane Junior School

GOING THROUGH TIME

It is good being an Egyptian you probably wonder why,
They built tall, tall pyramids that almost touch the sky.
It is good to be a Victorian you probably wonder why,
The Wright Brothers were the first people to fly,
It is good being a 20th century person you probably wonder why.
They build sky scrapers so very high.

Adam Lippett (10) Sandy Lane Junior School

WORLD WAR 3

I'm alone in the war. My mum and dad
are very poor.
Fighters, bombers flying around. Nuclear
bombs hit them to the ground.
Everyone is hurt in their heart or on
their body.
People risking their lives for their country to stay
in one piece alive or dead.

Neil McAlees (11) Sandy Lane Junior School

STAR MY PONY

She runs free in the field
That's my lovely pony
Head held high
Tail down low
And away she goes.

Sian Dempsey (9) Sandy Lane Junior School

FOOTBALL

Football is fun
Football is cool
I like it most
When I play it at school
Goals are scored in every game
Every team has a name
There's the FA every year to be won
Playing football is really fun.

Chris Anderson (9) Sandy Lane Junior School

CHAIR LIFT

I was standing on a yellow square
and suddenly the chair came.
Then I was sitting down and a bar came
over my head.
I was going up, up and up, I had one hand
on the bar.
Then I saw we were going down, down, down.
Then the bar come over my head again.
Run to the right the man said, so I did.
When I got off I said it was great!

Rosemary Modi (10) Sandy Lane Junior School

HOMELESS

I am cold and wet,
I feel so scared and thin,
all I have eaten from is tin,
I am dirty and helpless,
every bit of me is shaking,
All my toys were burnt,
but at least I have my freedom.

Sarah De Caux (8) Sandy Lane Junior School

HOMELESS

I'm smelly and stinky, cold, wet.
With a thin wet blanket half covering me!
I'm as hungry and thirsty as any
one can be.
But all I can do is suck
my thumb and hope for happiness
to come to me.

David Garstang (8) Sandy Lane Junior School

RUBBISH

Rubbish Rubbish in the air
Rubbish Rubbish everywhere
Rubbish in the playground
Rubbish in the school
Rubbish in the classroom
Rubbish in the hall
Rubbish Rubbish everywhere
Pick it up don't leave it there.

Hollie Roach (10) Sandy Lane Junior School

MY FAMILY

First I'll start with my mum,
Sits out there in the sun,
hands on her face, staring into space,
that is my mum.

Secondly comes my dad,
He is so mean and mad,
he moans day after day, standing in the way,
that is my dad.

Next comes Emily,
She's always getting uppity,
she tantrums all day long, never stops to sing a song,
that is Emily.

Next comes Grace,
Who's got the cheekiest face,
always getting into trouble, never at the double,
that is Grace.

Next comes Harriet,
She swings and shout a lot,
maybe one day, she'll learn how to play,
that is Harriet.

Next comes me,
as perfect as can be,
Never in trouble, always at the double,
that is me.

Laura Bryant (9) Sandy Lane Junior School

SPAGHETTI

Spaghetti Spaghetti
Twirls round my fork,
Spaghetti Spaghetti
To you I will talk.
Spaghetti Spaghetti
Goes well with Bolognaise
Spaghetti Spaghetti
Don't go well with Mayonnaise.

Bryn Chainey (9) Sandy Lane Junior School

HEIGHTS

I walk up the steep stairs
Not to look down
I'm nearly there at the top
Not to look down
I'm there I'm there I'm at the top
I look down
Oh no get me down
My dog comes near I jump
I look down again
Help I yell
Not to look down
I run down the steep stairs
I'm at the bottom
Not to look down

Bianka Roberts (10) Sandy Lane Junior School

LITTER

We are animals crawling on the floor.
Some of us eat insects now.
But sometimes we crawl into an empty
crisp packet and suffocate.
And it's all your fault that suddenly our
lives come to a halt.
Why do you litter?
Use the bins.
Is it a race?
That the first one to kill us wins.

Mark Wilson (10) Sandy Lane Junior School

COLOURS OF THE COUNTRYSIDE

In the yellow fields of corn,
Beautiful colours.
The orange and yellow sun comes up,
As the coloured cock crows in the morn.
The multi-coloured fields with sheep in,
Everything is as quiet as a mouse.
The sun starts to set,
As the sky goes orange, yellow and red like fire;
The white moon comes up and the stars
Twinkle.

Gillian Underdown (9) Sandy Lane Junior School

CRYSTAL SPRING

Crystal springs are crystal clear
There are strong animals like the bear
Cornfields swaying in the breeze
Birds are gathering in the trees
Buffaloes gathering into herds
It's lovely just to watch the birds
Wildlife must be lovely
From the great big elephant to the bumble bee.

Robin Lindsay-Kipp (9) Sandy Lane Junior School

THE DENTIST

I'm sitting there in my chair,
The dentist comes to give me a scare,
I see the drill come towards me,
It felt like I've cut my knee,
He looked at me long and hard,
My throat got solid just like lard,
Oh help help,
I pray so hard
He wonders why I'm going to cry
I tell him that I should die
I'm going to get out of here,
That's not a lie!

Rachel Muttock (10) Sandy Lane Junior School

MY TWO CATS

I have two cats,
Called Frank and Fluff,
They are both black,
And very tough.
They stand on guard,
In my yard,
When the neighbour's cats come in sight,
They offer them a fight,
But when they're indoors with me,
They're as friendly as can be.

Siobhan Stapleton (9) Sandy Lane Junior School

POWER RANGERS

I like Power Rangers
It's my favourite programme
On television
I never miss an episode
I like the Thunder Zords
Especially Tiger Zord
My television would have to break
For me to miss it!
When Power Rangers is on
I sit quietly watching the television
And shut my brother out of the room
Because he's always jumping around
Like a loony!
I like Power Rangers!

Lee Nicholls (9) Sandy Lane Junior School

PETS

My dad owns a pet shop so do I
full of insects and snakes of surprise
I have little gold fish swimming in tanks too
we have little puppies as cute as you
we have two parrots they sit on your arm
you have fun with them too

You have fun in the pet shop

Kerri Evanson (9) Sandy Lane Junior School

PUPPY DOG

If I had a wish,
I'd win the lottery,
I would buy a puppy dog,
For everyone to see,
I would love my puppy dog,
And I would sit and play,
I would kiss it and cuddle it,
And make it want to stay.

Laura Keeble (9) Sandy Lane Junior School

CONSERVATION

Red, yellow, pink, green, are all the colours in the rainbow,
Lovely fields of green, glistening in the sun,
Flowers swaying, bowing to one another,
Butterflies flying all around,
Animals drinking from a crystal clear spring,
The golden sunset, making the hills go red,
Echoes bouncing off the cliffs of the ocean
Roaring, the seabird cries.

Mark Newell (9) Sandy Lane Junior School

MY HAT IN THE WIND

I was in my garden on a windy day
And my hat blew off
    Oh No!
I tried to catch it but it blew away
And it blew over the fence
    Oh No!
I ran to the house and knocked on the door
But no-one came
    Oh No!
They must be out I said to myself
So I sadly went back home
    Oh No!
I went up stairs and into my room
And there was my hat sitting on my bed
    Oh Yes!

Tanya Swain (9) Sandy Lane Junior School

THE BLACK STALLION

Thundering through the dark, shady wood
The starless night sky
Hear the echo from the booms of the
regular beat
The roar of the wind screaming by
The crackle of the sticks underneath me
My body is as black as coal
Slower and slower and slower I get
because I have reached my halt.

Katy Hanbury (10) Sandy Lane Junior School

RUBBISH

I went outside and looked around
lots of rubbish on the ground.

Bottles, cans on the floor
it all looks very poor.

Horrible, revolting, nasty, yuck
it all looks like a lump of muck.

Litter is grubby, litter is smelly,
litter is the packets of things in your belly.

This is the message I am sending to you
Clean up your rubbish

Sean Cahill (10) Sandy Lane Junior School

WHAT IS RED?

Red is a rose that shines
in the sun. Red is the
colour of my heart.
Sometimes it shines
on my cheeks, when
I am embarrassed.
Red is a colour
of the rainbow
and red means
love.

Rachel Ward (8) Sandy Lane Junior School

THE DARK

As the dark is growing upon you
You hear the whistling wind blowing.
The light is turned into dark.
Oh No what's going on.
The light can't go just yet
It's only 7 o'clock.
It can only go when I go to bed.
And that's not going to be just yet.
You hear the owl going oo,oo and other noises too.
But in the morning
Where's all the dark gone it has turned back into light
I sing I shout I dance about.
Oh No I say to myself later,
The dark will be coming
And the light will be going.

Twyla Melanie Holland (9) Sandy Lane Junior School

THE BLITZ!

Being in the *blitz*
Must have been terrible.
People getting killed.
Aeroplanes getting shot down *bang!*
Being in the *blitz*
Must have been terrible.
We hope we never have to experience it
Shaking up and down and around.
O what a horrible world

Joe Keefe (10) Sandy Lane Junior School

HOLIDAYS

I went to Portugal on the plane,
When we got there it started to rain.
But after a day it was really sunny,
My uncle was telling jokes that were very funny.
When we were there,
It was really unfair.
My sisters got lots of lollies,
I had to push the trolleys!
We went to the beach every day,
Roy and I played in the sea.
When we were at the villa,
We went in the swimming pool.
Then we went home on the plane,
When we got home it started to
Rain rain rain rain rain.

Sarah Symes (10) Sandy Lane Junior School

RUBBISH

Rubbish rubbish everywhere
If you pick some up don't touch your hair
Rubbish on the pavement rubbish in the road
Where ever you look there is a load
If you have rubbish don't throw it on the floor
If you do you make even more
Drink cans and plastic bags
And lots of clothes all in rags

Lianne Osborn (10) Sandy Lane Junior School

FOOD

Food is very scrumptious
Especially chocolate cake,
Chocolate bars make you hungry
When you see them
It really seems very silly
But now I've got a tummy ache
Everyone is laughing
Because I ate too much
Now I'll never eat chocolate
again

Emma Blackall (10) Sandy Lane Junior School

PARENTS

Do your parents say,
Come here, go there.
Do they ever care?
Do this, do that,
Do I ever get time to sit on the mat?
Soon we're going on holiday
But did I ever get a say?
Parents can be anywhere,
Here, there, I mean everywhere.
Feed the fish, feed the cat.
All I say is . . .
I don't want to do that!

Ben Pocock (10) Sandy Lane Junior School

THE DENTIST

As I walk through the door
and hear my name called.
I sit on the chair and think help Lord.
They are horrible scary
they want to take you to bits
When I go to the dentist I feel down in the pits.
The nurse gives the tools to the dentist lady
She looks in my mouth and she murmurs *humm
well maybe.*
I feel as if I have no teeth
and she says well done and presses
the button underneath.

Kylie Taylor (9) Sandy Lane Junior School

MACHINES

*M*achines driving round the factory
   bang! bong! cling! clong!
*A*ll machines working through day and
   night,
*C*all of a man who said, 'Go home
   good night don't let the bed bugs
   bite.'
*H*alt all the vehicles I've got to
   check them through,
I turned all the robots off,
*N*othing left to do.
*E*verything was quiet in the mist
   of the night,
*S*unset behind the trees,
   Machines must wait till first light.

Adam Minns (9) Sandy Lane Junior School

AIR RAID

I was sitting in my bedroom
almost asleep
When I heard a single noise
It brought me to my feet.
It was like a blare of thunder
Then it died down
My body froze my heart drowned
It was followed by a siren
too deafening to hear
It brought a little ache
To my little ear
I ran to the door
and opened it with fear
It made me a lot happier
When I saw my mum was near.
She hurried us downstairs
across the kitchen floor
out in the garden
through the shelter door.
The next sound was the worst to come
It sounded like a big loud drum
Then the siren sounded again
We opened the door and saw lots of men.
They were the men from the ARP
We discussed the damage over a pot of tea.

Jemma Parsons (11) Sandy Lane Junior School

WHAT WENT ON IN THE WAR

What I can see,
is very frightening,
I must tell you,
this awful thing,
First some sound,
then some light,
the sky went red,
what a fright,
some screams,
some shouts,
cries of people,
with some doubts,
I pray today,
that we will survive,
from the pilotless planes,
and very big bombs,
people sheltering with a horrid look,
It feels real horrid,
to you in this way today.

Sam Wortley (10) Sandy Lane Junior School

LITTER

Pollution's really rather bad
Dumping rubbish makes me sad
Instead of looking in the sky
Pick up rubbish as you walk by
Otherwise I'll be very mad
Because you're making the world bad

Michael Drury (10) Sandy Lane Junior School

THE VICTORIANS

We have burgers, beans and chips
Victorians had salted beef and bits,

They had to work in mines
While we enjoy spending lucky dimes,

Their clothes were very different
Wear clothes like that we couldn't,

Victorians were very poor
Having to walk across the soggy moor,

They all lived in cottages
But they had no riches,

Their kitchens and that were made of stone
and their gardens were never mown.

Sean Knight (10) Sandy Lane Junior School

HOMELESS

I feel cold dirty dehydrated
A thin blanket that is wet.
It doesn't feel very good
We are hungry
Smelly and wet. Will this hunger end?
I have no clothes
I am lost
and lonely.

Joseph Winters (8) Sandy Lane Junior School

CHEMISTRY

I'm really into chemistry,
because it's such a mystery
The Bunsen burner is so much fun,
experiments there are more than one.
Creating this creating that
within this subject there is so much fact.
Lotions, potions, creams and gels,
and many many horrid smells.
Caution and care is all that's needed
assistance now the professor pleaded.

Frank Neville (9) Sandy Lane Junior School

VISIT TO THE PARK

Today I went cycling
In the park
I saw some dogs
Who started to bark
We bought an ice-cream
From the van
We have to eat it
As fast as we can
The sun was shining in the sky
I saw a plane
Which was flying high
We walked round the lake
A very long way
We must have walked
Three miles today!

Rachel Martin (9) Sandy Lane Junior School

FOOTBALL

Football is the game to play
Scoring goals along the way
Strikers, forwards, midfield too
All the fans they cheer and boo

Arsenal, Chelsea, Man U too
But it is Spurs we shout, we love you
With our matching kit and waving scarves
We come to see our favourite stars.

Stephen Pilkington (8) Sandy Lane Junior School

THE CAR TRIP

Mum says
'Right you two this is a long journey
I'm driving and I can't drive properly if
you go mad OK'
'Yes mam we say'
off we go . . .
The moaning starts, 'He's playing with the door
now.'
'Can I open my window?'
'He's spitting.'
'Look there's a tree says mum.'
And the moaning starts again
'Are we nearly there? Don't pull my hair.'
Mum says,
'I'm stopping the car if you don't stop it
to throw you out.'
'OK mum we say . . .
Can I have a drink?'

Andrew Rouse (9) Sandy Lane Junior School

HOMEWORK

I've got to do my homework
I've got to have it done

I've got to do my homework
before I have some fun

I've got to do my homework
It's just not any fun

And now I've done my homework
It's time the fun begun.

Darren Tibby (9) Sandy Lane Junior School

CHARLOTTE

Charlotte is sometimes bossy
Sometimes cute.
Charlotte is sometimes sweet
Sometimes stressy
She breaks up with me
She shouts at me
But we're best friends
Like friends should be

Some say Charlie Farlie
Some just plain Charlie
I prefer Charlie myself
I don't know about her
But we're best friend like
Friends should be
Me and Charlie you see.

Enrica Stevens (9) Sandy Lane Junior School

WORKING SO HARD FOR NOTHING

I was making a brilliant present for my mum,
Sweat running down my face.
Sawing, drilling, sanding and hammering for my mum,
Mother's Day tomorrow still got lots to do.

Working hard
Working working
Working hard for nothing!

Can't stop for a break
Got to get this present done
Almost there now finished
Mum's going to really like this present

Working hard
Working working
Working hard for nothing!

What a work of art
Look at these curves
Look at that painting
Crafted by my own hand

Working hard
Working working
Working hard for nothing!

I gave it to my mum the next day
She just said thank you and what is it
She didn't even recognise wooden flowers
All that work for nothing!

Michael Reading (10) Sandy Lane Junior School

THE BIG WHEEL

A stomach-churner
A heart-pounder
A blood-pumper
A hair-raiser
A knuckle-whitener
A lung-strainer
A body-shaker
An eye-stretcher
A mouth-opener

Mark Evans (11) Sandy Lane Junior School

AUSTRALIA

North, South, East or West
Australia's the place your love best
In the West there's Gibson's desert
Where the sand is hot and not very
pleasant.
In the North, there's the great
Barrier Reef.
Where the fish roam free
In the South there's Tasmania
an island bigger than Romania
In the East lies the Jewels
in the Crown
The capital Canberra can be
found
Sydney with the 8th Wonder of
the World
The magnificent building of
The Opera House.

Marcia Peterson (9) Sandy Lane Junior School

THE BLITZ

First the calm, dark night,
Stillness creeping all around,
Everybody deep in slumber,
No-one moving, not a mouse,
Sleeping, sleeping, sleeping,

The drone of planes overhead,
The slow buzz of the bombers,
No-one there to hear the noise,
Like giant bees with giant stings,
Humming, humming, humming,

Then a flash lights up the sky,
Screams cutting through the air like knives,
Panic, confusion, blood, sweat and fire,
In the mad dash to get away,
Screaming, screaming, screaming,

Afterwards the silence again,
The terrible silence of death,
Creeping round the once-was village,
With only flames flickering into the night,
Dying, dying, dying.

Ruth Brooks (11) Sandy Lane Junior School

POLLUTION

Government and industry let's find a sollution
Let's get rid of this deadly pollution
Cases of asthma is on the rise
Which really comes as no surprise
Carbon Monoxide, smog and smoke
Help to get rid of this pollution or we will all choke.

Ashleigh Handley (10) Sandy Lane Junior School

SUMMER

In the summer sun
We have lots of fun,
Playing in the sand hand in hand
Buckets and spades
Bats and balls
Lots of games for us all.
Fish and chips by the sea
Lollies and ice-creams,
Maybe a cup of tea
This is how we have fun in the
Lovely summer sun.

Laura Wortley (9) Sandy Lane Junior School

MY SHADOW

My shadow,
It follows me around all day,
If the sun is out,
All I can say is,
It is usually about.

Always black,
Behind my back,
With no eyes,
Or nose.

So as you can see,
My shadow is really,
A black picture,
Of me!

Rebecca Durbin (10) Sandy Lane Junior School

SNOW

Snow is white
As white as can be
As clear as day
So you can see
It falls heavy
And it falls light
Snow is a truly lovely sight
When it snows in my garden
I jump for joy
Girls just cry
But I'm a boy
I make big snowballs
To throw at my dad
He takes so much
And says, 'That's enough lad.'
The following day
When the sun comes out
I really feel
Like I want to shout
Go away sun
Don't dry it up
I try to collect the remains in a cup!

John Knight (9) Sandy Lane Junior School

THE LION

He stalks through the jungle
night and day.
He wonders round to find his prey.
He lies down low
and with one ginormous leap.
He knocks the startled creature
right off his feet.
Satisfied at last.

Terry Devine (11) Sandy Lane Junior School

THE DENTIST

I get nervous when I go
they want to take my teeth out but I say no
they give me stickers and some nice sweets
but I say no I don't want their treats
I feel sick and want to go home
but sitting there I feel like a garden gnome
when they say my teeth are fine,
I get home and look in the mirror I see them shine

Elisa Coleman (10) Sandy Lane Junior School

BABY PARYS

I couldn't contain my joy
That you where a girl and not a boy
You are small like a doll
Not noisy at all
With hair that is red
and eyes now brown
You sleep in your bed
When you cry you frown
You're quiet and sweet
You're perfect and neat
You've made my dream come true
and I'm uncle Harry to you.

Harry Levey (10) Sandy Lane Junior School

MY SPECIAL PET

One day I went to the pet shop to buy
a special pet.
To cuddle him and squeeze him they
did not have it yet.
So then I came to get him one day.
I promised to love him in a very
special way.
He handed me a box and so I looked
inside.
His big fluffy tail he really could not
hide!
I found my little rabbit as cute as
can be.
My very special rabbit - meant only
for me.

Jenni Day (8) Sandy Lane Junior School

MY LITTLE SISTER

A hair-puller,
An arm-pincher,
An ankle-kicker,
A homework-messer,
A clothes-ruiner,
A knee-scraper,
A pet-killer,
A room-messer,
A total nightmare.

Alex Pobgee (11) Sandy Lane Junior School

THE DAMAGE OF THE WORLD

The world is dead,
I'm lying in bed,
We hear the engines starting up,
Mum sighs and puts down her cup,
The sirens start to whirr and whirr,
I start to cry, my eyes blur,
Won't it ever stop?

The noise gets louder and louder still,
I fell giddy and then ill,
I run towards the Anderson Shelter,
Everyone's running helter skelter,
Won't it ever stop?

The door opens and then slams shut,
I'm inside now but:
The pain's still there and people too,
Alison, George, Sarah and Drew,
Won't it ever stop?

Outside the noises are still going on,
Shouting, screaming, the dropping of bombs,
Echoing around and around my head,
It's so scary I feel like I'm dead,
Won't it ever stop?

Eventually I fall asleep,
Dreaming of things I don't want to meet,
Hitler, bombs and things like that,
I wake up with a jerk, something's not quite right,
I look out of the window, what a terrible sight,
I step back, what a shock, what a fright,
Won't it ever stop?

Houses burnt down,
People are crying,
Some are dead,
Some are dying,

Won't it ever stop?

Frances Carr & Hannah Morris (11) Sandy Lane Junior School

BEING THE OLDEST

I'm the oldest in my family
And I get very sad
My brother and my sisters
They always drive me mad

They get away with murder
While I get doom and gloom
And all my father shouts at me is

Go and clean your room

They always mess my toys up
And they mess up my life
Oh why am I the oldest?
Oh why Oh why Oh why?

But I guess I get more money
And I always get new clothes
So maybe things are not so bad
But that's the way life goes.

Charlotte Gaskin (9) Sandy Lane Junior School

DAYS

Mondays I watch 'Next of Kin'.
Tuesdays I watch 'CITV'.
Wednesdays I go to choir.
Thursdays I go in the garden and
        play football.
Fridays I watch 'Due South'.
Saturdays I might go fishing.
Sundays I get ready to go back to
        school the next day.

Alex Keefe (9) Sandy Lane Junior School

THE WHITE DOVE

Look out there
Look above.
And you should see
The great white Dove.
His black eye spying.
His white wing flapping.
The dove has come to rest
On an old wood fence.
The dove has gone to mate.

Zhala Jordan (8) Shaw-Cum-Donnington School

SATS

I heard about SATS and gasped
but I then just forgot
I should have prepared earlier
I tried my hardest
but was it enough?
I envy clever people
I envy that they don't struggle
pressure
I struggled
worry, strain
those SATS made me a nervous wreck
the pursuit was too much
and when I get the results back, will it show?

Joanna Rhoderick (11) St Mary's School, Mortimer

THE BUS SHELTER

The number 169 to London , leaves,
The last bus,
Only the tramp sits in the bus shelter,
His room for the night,
All he's got is a thin blanket,
The wind howls,
One of the windows is broken,
Not at all safe,
Not at all secure,
Lonely, as the sun goes down.

Inneka Evans (10) St. Mary's School, Mortimer

THE TOMATO SALAD

Being buried,
Hidden from light,
Creatures crawling round my feet.
Suddenly the ceiling comes in,
Sunlight breaks through,
The seed shatters,
I emerge from the undergrowth,
Swaying to and fro.
I ripen a brilliant red,
As the sun tans my flesh,

A giant figure,
plucks me from my home,
A sharp cold blade,
Slices me,
Shredding my flesh,
dropped, plunging down,
into a mass of green leaves,
Laying quite silent,
ripped apart,
My soul is drained.

Hannah St Paul (11) St Mary's School, Mortimer

A HOMELY HOME

Bricks, cement, wood and glass,
Put together firm and fast,
People going,
People coming,
Curtains, carpets,
Beds and spreads.
A country lane runs right past
A house is a home when it's yours.

Charlotte Haines (11) St Mary's School, Mortimer

HADES

Entering the dark chamber of spirits and death
Lifeless and empty.
The reeking smell of decaying bodies,
The eerie quietness of floating souls,
A dark pool of sacrificial blood lies thick.
Murky, dull darkness of Hades!
Cave of death.

Rupert Hetherington (11) St Mary's School, Mortimer

A HOME IS WHERE THE HEART IS

When a house is built
It is not a home.
A house is made of brick and stone,
A home is where the heart is.

The place where prized possessions keep,
where emotions live, to laugh then weep.
A house is made of brick and stone
A home is where the heart is.

A house is empty and then filled,
Gadgets and furniture scattered around.
A house is made of brick and stone
A home is where the heart is.

In World War II
Most had the home,
But not the house,
Their life contained in the London underground.
A house is made of brick and stone,
But, a home is where the heart is.

Rosie Wilkin (11) St Mary's School, Mortimer

MY HOME IS MY OWN

My home is my own
It has been all the time
Although appearance, rather small
To me it's grand and fine
Not just three bedrooms
A kitchen, a bathroom
A living room and garden too
What is a cosy home to me
Is just a house to you
I have my clothes, toys and games
And precious things to keep near
But think of the homeless
I'm sure they'd shed a tear
If only those in ragged clothes
And barefooted, dirty tramps
Could know the joy and comfort of
Possessions that are their own

Rachel Overett (11) St Mary's School, Mortimer

THE HEALTHY AND THE HOMELESS

The homeless,
Curled up in a cardboard box
Shivering from the cold.
Us in our warm houses
Stretched out in front of the fire,
Cosy and warm.

All they have is a tiny rug to cover them,
A couple of belongings which are very precious to them,
While we have duvets and blankets,
And a million toys compared to them.
How they long to live like us,
To them we are like royalty.

Sitting in a corner pale and frightened
Nothing to eat for two days,
Then a stale piece of bread and a cup of water,
They are like spiders waiting to be stepped on.
We are on the sofa watching TV
Having had a proper meal,
Taking everything for granted.

We have a home,
They have nothing.

Melanie Hillyard (11) St. Mary's School, Mortimer

MYSTERY CAT

The church clock strikes a quarter to midnight,
From beneath the shadows something stirs,
A slim sleek cat appears,
Its body as black as coal,
Its eyes sparkling dangerously,
Moonlight softly filters through the clouds,
The air around is hot and humid,
Gracefully the cat leaps up onto a dustbin,
And begins to purr , creating a rich mellow sound,
Her purring is interrupted by an unwanted noise,
She jumps swiftly up to an iron railing,
And disappears into the deep shadows.

Philippa Bell (10) St Mary's School, Mortimer

A SIMILE POEM

I was in a field of fluorescent green,
Full of golden daffodils.
As if they were ballerinas dancing in yellow frilled
Dresses they swayed from side to side in the breeze
of a sunny day.
The sun was like a golden face of flames,
Looking at me from far above.
The trees were like lime flavoured ice creams,
with flakes of dust sparkling like ice on a pavement
of frost.
The distant songs from far above, from birds flying
Like a cloud of feathers as if they were happy,
I was listening to their songs of beauty.
The hills of patchwork were like a blanket of wool
on a king size bed,

Jolene Taylor (11) St Mary's CE Junior School, Thatcham

A FAR AWAY LAND

There's a far away valley over the hills and at the end of the rainbow.
Where the beautiful carpet stretches over the land.
Where the dinosaurs play in a land beyond time.
Where trees in the meadow sway like a wonderful kite.
And the horses run free like a leaf dancing in the wind.
Where the unicorns sing like a choir of children.
And the birds whistle softly like the wind and the breeze.
Where the reindeers drink in the lake like the sky.
And now it is night time the stars twinkle high, like a stretched pattern.
Then the animals lie in the field, not forgotten.

Emily Barker (11) St Mary's CE Junior School, Thatcham

LOST PARADISE

When I looked at the world, I saw . . .
An abysmal sight,
In the middle of the night.

When I looked at the world, I saw . . .
A serious story,
Disgusting and gory.

When I looked at the world I saw . . .
Treason,
Without reason.

When I looked at the world I saw . . .
Unbelievable gloom, Murder and doom.

When I looked at the world I saw . . .
A cheap and loathsome place,
In an empty space.

When I looked at the world I thought . . .
If we all work together
We can change this place,
Together we'll be one smiling, happy face!

Emily Clarke (11) St Mary's CE Junior School, Thatcham

THE HOPELESS FLIGHT

I bow my head in sorrow,
At the beginning she was pure,
But now this world is stale,
I cry for her once more.
I cry because I killed her,
You may not even care,
But she cared about the animals.
As bright as the sun reflected on a
Mirror was she,
I wanted to keep it a secret but
I supposed you've already guessed,
Her name was Mother Nature,
She was the best.
She tried to help us start again,
To put all wrongs to right,
But she did not win,
She lost the hopeless
Fight.

Rachel Manser (11) St Mary's CE School, Thatcham

WORLD DESTRUCTION

If you take a breath
Of the poisoned air,
Someone will weep over your death,
Somewhere out there.

All because of man,
A deadly machine,
He polluted the world,
It might never be clean.

He hunts the whale,
But will always fail,
For Greenpeace is there
To stop him!

Lindsey Edwards (10) St Mary's CE Junior School, Thatcham

A CHILD'S CHRISTMAS THOUGHTS

I hear the bells chiming in the distance.
As we put decorations on the dark green tree,
It started to snow.
As I looked out of the window
My eyes twinkled to see
That pure white snow settle on the floor
It was magic.
As I went to bed
I had sugar plums dancing in my head.
Finally it was going to be covered in white snow outside.
In the morning
I open my presents.
I'm jolly careful not to ruin the beautiful Christmas paper,
that's been beautifully wrapped.
Mum gets to start on the turkey.
Grandad and granny are coming to eat,
And they're bringing my present.
I think the best part of Christmas
Is presents.

Cara Hawkes (10) St Mary's Primary School, Winkfield

THE SUN

Shining blazing golden ball,
Sitting there doing nothing at all.
Golden ball, What are you?
You are as gold as gold can be
Sitting on a bright blue sea.
When I wake up, you give a welcoming sight
Because you shine so beautifully bright.

Claire Hipkin (8) St Mary's Primary School, Winkfield

VE DAY POEM

Victory in Europe announced Winston Churchill,
End of the war on May the 8th,
Dropping of bombs ceased,
And everywhere there were celebrations,
Yet there was silence for 2 minutes.

Celebrations started again 50 years later,
Everywhere in Europe people died fighting for King and country,
Let this be remembered for years to come,
Even us young,
But why should we celebrate?
Really we should because of the efforts
And the lives that were lost,
Trying to free us from Hitler,
In the war years,
On every battle ground in the air, on the sea and land,
No man is ever to be forgotten who fought in the war.
So I think we should celebrate what happened 50 years ago.

Timothy Zacks (11) St Mary's Primary School, Winkfield

A WINDY DAY

A breeze has come.
It changes to a wind like flames getting bigger.
It starts to get stronger and harder,
'Til it gets really rough!
A hurricane comes, then a tornado!
Pulling roofs off houses wrecking everything.
Trees out of the ground.
People floating in mid air.

Clare Fisher (8) St Mary's Primary School, Winkfield

THE BEGINNING AND END

Blue sky
Green earth
Coloured flowers
Coloured birds

Pink pigs
Chestnut horses
Black ants
Gruffing dogs

Black people
Pink people
Yellow people
Coloured people

Calamity
Gases
Disaster
Nothing

Samantha Whitfield (11) St Mary's Primary School, Winkfield

VE DAY

A time when guns blared in the streets
A time when destruction ruled the cities
A time when widows weep and weep
When they find their loved ones are not coming home.
Then a time for celebration and peace.
People having street parties
Fireworks going off
The queen making a speech.
50 years on, we are still remembering that day
And all those brave people who died for us and our country.

Andrew Park (11) St Mary's Primary School, Winkfield

DAYDREAMS

Mrs Jeffery thinks I'm reading
but I'm not.
I'm having a war
girls against boys
and girls are winning.
I'm doing a
double-backwards somersault,
I'm flying up high
with my own wings,
I'm in the netball match
playing GA,
and I'm scoring
all the goals.
Stop it, stop it,
Oh no, the class is empty
There's only me.

Clare Coughlan (10) St Mary's Primary School, Winkfield

BOARDING SCHOOL

First day at a new school.
I don't know anyone.
People laughing.
Having fun.
There's a person I'd like to meet.
Now she's my friend
At boarding school
At boarding school.

Sarah Badham-Thornhill (9) St Mary's Primary School, Winkfield

A CARPET OF BLUEBELLS

It's spring and the bluebells
are all around
how beautiful they look
there in the ground.

A carpet of bluebells
a lovely sight
especially when the
sun's shining bright.

A couple of rabbits
dodging around, in a
thrilling dark blue
sea they've found.

The bluebells lift their
heads to the trees
and sway together in
the warm, soft breeze.

Bethan Denman (10) St Mary's Primary School, Winkfield

TWO CATS

Two cats together on a very hot day.
Two cats together that play all day.
Two cats together that go home for tea.
Two cats together are scared of the sea.
Two cats together go to bed.
Two cats together think it's raining
Or is it just my brain.
Two cats dream of lots of hot days, all night long.

Jessica Williams (8) St Mary's Primary School, Winkfield

DAYDREAMS

Mrs Jeffrey thinks I'm
reading but
I'm wondering what is happening in space
and here and there

Mrs Jeffery thinks
I'm working
but she's
wrong of course
I'm racing in the
Grand National and my one's
the only horse
I'm coming up
to the finishing line
and I won
obviously
Suddenly!
I find that everyone is looking at
me and
it's my turn to read.

David Kayser (9) St Mary's Primary School, Winkfield

VE DAY

I stand around
Surrounded by red, white, and blue costumes
Celebrations with plenty of food
Sirens go on and off all day
at the schools
Children have the Union Jack flag
and little hats
Children laugh and play

We remember 50 years ago
When all those people went to war
We won and we are happy
but we have to remember
the people who died
fighting for us.

Laura Jane Bartlett (10) St Mary's Primary School, Winkfield

VE DAY

My heart breaks
When I think of all the people
Who died in the war
but after all the sorrow
I think of happiness
Joy and street parties
Songs and music
lots of people having fun
celebrating VE day

Kirsten Jardine (10) St Mary's Primary School, Winkfield

V E DAY

Celebrating the end of the war
Thinking of those who died
People fighting for our country
Just throwing away their life.

People don't come home
Must have been scared
Having planes come closer
Just in case they drop
Bombs near.

Celebrating 50 years on
We have had peace so far
Having 2 minutes silence
We dress in blue, red and white.

Having big street parties
Having special VE day services
Talk to old people
About the war and
Asking what it was like
Coming home.

Jamie Barber (11) St Mary's Primary School, Winkfield

VE DAY

Band playing
People screaming with joy
Flags high in the sky
People in red, white and blue
Fireworks exploding in the air
All clear sirens going off
The two minute silence
To remember the people who died for us.

Ryan Jones (11) St Mary's Primary School, Winkfield

THE CLOUD

It's cold, it's cold!
The wind's coming in.
That means the clouds are coming.
They are grey and heavy.
Oh no!
It's starting to rain.
I run to the car, sleepy and cold.
When we get home the sun comes out
But when we go outside, the clouds come back.
Oh no!

Hayley Bolland   (8) St Mary's Primary School, Winkfield

VE DAY

Remembering the war
And those who died in fighting
Families killed in bombing
Celebrating victory
Having parties
Seeing fireworks light up the sky
Dancing
Union Jack flags waving
People celebrating
Remembering the war
And those who died in fighting
Families killed in bombing

Clare Powell (11) St Mary's Primary School, Winkfield

VE DAY

The end of the suffering
The end of the pain
Great celebrations everywhere
Then 50 years on
2 minutes go by in silence
As we think of the dead

People dress in red, white and blue
The street parties
Thousands of people there
Then beacons lit around the country
Celebrating our victory over Hitler

Tom Powell (11) St Mary's Primary School, Winkfield

VE DAY

50 years ago we won the war over Germany
50 years ago people played and celebrated in the streets.
50 years ago fireworks were set off and bonfires blared
50 years ago for once silence was in the air.
50 years ago Winston Churchill gave his famous speech
50 years ago Adolf Hitler committed suicide.
Now days we celebrate once more but
Still remember those who died for us and
fought for us.

Jack Tickner (11) St Mary's Primary School, Winkfield

VE DAY POEM

Why do we call it Victory in Europe Day?
When some people aren't celebrating
Because they've lost husbands and children.
Rrrr, the VI's fly over then complete
Silence, a split second after that, woo woo
woo, quick to the shelter.
That was just a bit to show how much suffering was suffered
but my own opinion is, it should be called
Victory in Europe day.

Lloyd Matthews (11) St Mary's Primary School, Winkfield

LILY

Your pink petals shine so bright,
Your friend the daisy is so light.
You close your petals every night.
To find the morning so bright,
what a shame you have to die.
How we will miss you,
every day and every night.

Helen Morton (10) St Mary's Primary School, Winkfield

FLOWERS

A little yellow buttercup is standing in the sun,
A red little tulip is shining in the sun,
Pink and red roses,
are having fun,
A daffodil is waving, shining in the breeze,
While the lily opens and
shows its lovely petals
Pink, white and blue.

Jennifer Hills (10) St Mary's Primary School, Winkfleld

RAIN

Oh no grey sky!
That means clouds
And clouds mean rain!
Rain makes me feel grim and bored
Because I love going outside and playing.
But I like rain as well,
I like splashing and seeing other people enjoying
themselves
Splish splosh splash!

Louise Ingham (8) St Mary's Primary School, Winkfield

RAIN

Oh no! I can see a big black cloud
It's starting to rain.
I'm soaking!
Drips and drops going through my rain-coat,
Put up your umbrella!
Put up your hood!
The sea is rising, water rising.
Lakes are rising,
Ducks are rising.

Naomi Kasaska (8) St Mary's Primary School, Winkfield

THUNDER AND LIGHTNING

I hear thunder.
I saw a flash of lightning, lots of cloud.
I jump and hide under shelter.
I'm cold.
I put my hood on.
It's like a giant thumping for his dinner.
I'm scared! Please stop! It's like drums banging.
Phew, it's stopped.

Cassie Cella (8) St Mary's Primary School, Winkfield

RAIN

Rain, rain, that's what we like!
Rain is wet
Rain is cold
Rain, rain, you're the best!
So rain rain rain come again!

Stuart Bennett (8) St Mary's Primary School, Winkfield

VE DAY

I remember the aeroplanes going by
I remember the old people standing high
I remember the street party going by
And best of all red, white and blue, that's why
Lasers are high in the sky.

Ryan Godding (10) St Mary's Primary School, Winkfield

VE DAY

Saddening sorrows with people dying.
Every day and every night.
Happy parties and celebrations.
Cakes and flags flying everywhere.
Laughing and crying remembering and celebrating
the war.
Trying to hold in the lives of people or loved ones
that have died.

Edward Cooper (10) St Mary's Primary School, Winkfield

VE DAY, 50 YEARS POEM

Veterans with all their medals
Excited families watching fireworks
During the war many people died
A two minute silence
Yelling, shouting and happiness

50,000 people died fighting for freedom
Ordinary, innocent people bombed
Yet, we're still celebrating?
Enormous loads of Jews tortured
And we still celebrate?
Rows of soldiers gave their lives
Still we celebrate?

Nicholas Chapman (11) St Mary's Primary School, Winkfield

BOMB

River all black,
Bomb in the air,
People and children,
Crying and screaming.
All in the dungeon.
Some in the war.
No people are safe,
The noise has stopped,
What's happening out there.
No bombs are firing,
No guns are shooting
The noise has stopped
Hurrah!

Francesca Heath (9) St Mary's Primary School, Winkfield

DAYDREAMS

Mrs Jeffery thinks I'm listening
to what I have to do.
But what am I really doing?
If only she knew!

I'm riding a giant condor,
floating with the breeze,
I'm swimming under water . . .
'Talli! Listen please!'
Another command from the teacher,
but here we go again!
I'm going to the future
in a brilliant time-machine!

I'm racing with an ostrich, then
Bang! It's all gone!
'Talli! You haven't done one sum yet!'
(But at least they aren't wrong!)

Talli Haim (10) St Mary's Primary School, Winkfield

VE DAY

People stand with red,
White and blue
Costumes.
There is music going on
and everybody sings.
You can hardly talk amongst yourselves.
The celebration goes on for ages.
We must remember 50 years ago
that the war was on
and many people died
Who fought for us.
We won and we are happy.

Sarah Colborn (11) St Mary's Primary School, Winkfield

SUMMER SUN

The sun shines brightly
It smells fresh and new.
Flowers wake up, it's the sun.
It's morning mum.
It's sunny, hooray, hooray,
I can't wait to go out and play.
I love the sun,
I love it.
Flowers are lovely,
A host of daffodils.
I would like one of them.
Summer sun, shine more,
A nice day to start the weekend.
This is lovely,
Please come again,
Summer sun.

Sarah Nagalewska (8) St Mary's Primary School, Winkfield

CLOUDS

Fluffy puffy white as snow,
Making pictures as they go.
Sailing by like cotton wool white and fluffy.

Watch out dark clouds hanging low,
Dull, smoky, making me miserable.

Like ghosts fluffy and white or dark and thick.

Emily Murphy (8) St Mary's Primary School, Winkfield

MY BLUEBELLS

I'm walking through the forest
On a beautiful summer's day,
Along a lovely blue carpet
Made with bluebells,
My bluebells.

They grow so wild,
There are millions of
them
They never stop
growing,
Not my bluebells,
Never will they stop
growing.

They're sometimes
Purpley blue,
Sometimes
Pinkey blue,
But my bluebells are
always beautiful to look at.

Laura Finnieston (10) St Mary's Primary School, Winkfield

FRIENDS

Friends are fun to have around,
Especially in the playground.
They help you when you fall,
They may be very tall,
They help you find,
They may be kind.
But you can always depend,
On a friend.

They help you in the classroom,
They may need to use the bathroom.
My friend is called Sarah,
She has a bear called Beara.
She writes with a pen,
She gets ten out of ten.
But you can always depend,
On a friend.

Laura Cronk (9) St Mary's Primary School, Winkfield

MY BIG BROTHER

My brother's olders than me
My brother has homework
My brother has friends round
My brother plays football

My brother snores at night
My brother eats like a pig
My brother's got a girlfriend
My brother goes to restaurants.

My Mum loves my
brother,
so does my Dad
And so do I

Not!

Amy Grainger (9) St Mary's Primary School, Winkfield

WINTER

Winter is a cold wave, washing colour out of the world,
Throwing hail and rain it has many times hurled,
Pulling leaves from bushes and trees,
With its strong winds bringing people to their knees,
Many creatures losing their homes,
Trees from the ground where the wood creature roams.

Mud ev'rywhere,
And the wind in your hair,
A hot stew in the dish,
For the boys out to fish,
Out to catch the roach and the chubb,
Then together their hands to keep warm they will rub.

The bells at the church so loudly will ring,
To mark end of winter, beginning of spring.

Peter Jones (11) Waltham St Lawrence School

WINTER

Trees in winter are bare, boring and brown.
Puddles creak, crackle and break under your feet.
White with frost the earth is hard and frosty.
Windy days when winter thunders through air.
Fog is damp, gloomy and misty not a thing you can see.
Hunters thunder through the bare and brown countryside.
The wind is roaring now, but the trees are just as boring.
Winter whips through the country wiping everything out.

Robert Taylor (10) Waltham St Lawrence School

THE JOY OF FREEDOM

In the corner of the field stands a horse.
Ears up, nostrils flared.
Eyes watching warily.
Its mane blows in the wind
As it lets out an ear-piercing whinny.
It shakes its head and snorts.
A startling noise
And the ears go back.
A shiver rippling through its satin skin.
It paces the field,
Watching, always watching.
A car goes past,
The horse turns,
And gallops down the field,
Mane and tail streaming behind.
Hooves leaving a path of dust.
It is approached by a human,
Who is holding a headcollar.
Again the ears are lowered.
The whinny is long and loud,
Before it rears, towering above the world.
It kicks its long legs
And descends to the ground,
In a flurry of hooves.
Then it stands watching as the human goes.
The horse is happy and rears again.
Only this time for a different reason.
The pure joy of freedom.

Helen Vincent (11) Whiteknights CP School

DEAD CAT

The cat lies there lifeless,
No glint left in the filmed, yellow eyes,
The soft fluffy fur matted,
Where the blood is still wet,
No-one knows about the death, except the careless driver in the road,
The sounds of life, now locked away by death,
The fur no longer a soft white, but now stained by red and brown,
No traces left by the guilty murderer, the cat paid the price,
I will never again feel that wet nose against my face,
Cruelty and death is endless

Julia Pike (11) Whiteknights CP School

A POEM ABOUT SCHOOL

I think school is really boring,
Most of the time I end up snoring.
History really is the worst,
So much info I almost burst.
Lunch, break and home time is cool,
I'll push the teachers in the pool.
You get to see your friends every day,
But only in play.
For five days you work all day,
Don't you think you should get paid.
PE really is the best,
But after this you need a rest.
When you get home you're bored stiff,
And to top it up you and your brother have a tiff
I think school is really boring
When it's over, I wake up yawning.

Andrew Walter (10) Whiteknights CP School

ONE DREADFUL NIGHT

In the middle of the night,
When there isn't any light,
And everyone's asleep,
So there's no one that will speak,
Out come the ghosts,
Mainly dead TV hosts,
They host their TV shows,
And nobody ever knows,
That is up until now,
When only I allow,
To let you know,
That I've seen one of their shows,
It was on one dreadful night,
That I got my big fright,
It was about 12 o'clock,
And my cover had just slipped off,
I did a great big sigh,
And turned on to my side,
Then something appeared,
So I started to jeer,
They took me roughly by my hands,
And tied me up with rubber bands,
It made me watch its TV show,
And then thank God he let me go,
I'll never forget that dreadful night,
When someone gave me such a fright.

Aimee Driscoll (10) Whiteknights CP School

OLD MEMORIES

He sat there, motionless,
Dreaming of the world to come,
Dreaming of the morning sun,
Seventy three,
And waiting for some company.

The doorbell rang,
Such joys ran through his mind,
of wondrous people to greet, he'll find,
He answered the door,
to a mate from the Second World War.

He'd make some coffee,
for his old co-pilot Tommy,
They'd chat about the times they'd had,
The ones which were good and the ones
which were bad.

For King and Country,
He wanted to do what was best,
he then felt sorrow for those
that were laid down to rest.

Victoria Joslin (11) Whiteknights CP School

AN AUTUMN CYCLE RIDE

Out of the town,
Wind in my face,
Just a leisurely bike ride,
There's no race.

Leaves flutter,
To the ground,
A completely,
Desolate sound.

People having,
A picnic lunch,
I cycle over the leaves,
I think the word 'scrunch'.

Into the town,
Smog in the air,
Cars all around,
Getting nowhere.

Engines revving,
Exhaust fumes choking.
The anxious drivers,
Awaiting a right turning.

Thomas Green (10) Whiteknights CP School

DAYDREAMING

As I sit in the classroom,
Staring into space,
I imagine myself in my own little place.

Ignoring everything the teacher says,
I'm booking my holidays with A T Mays.

I'm on the plane to Walt Disney World,
Sitting next to someone whose hair is curled.

Going on the rides, this is fun.
I've got butterflies in my tum.

Wake up! Wake up! The teacher says,
You're having one of your daydreaming days.

David Morgan (11) Whiteknights CP School

HOMEWORK

Homework every Friday,
Hand it in on Wednesday,
What's the point,
We do enough at school,
Work work,
At school,
At home,
Who invented homework,
If only I knew,
I would prefer to watch a video,
Anything's better than homework,
It's time for Superman on TV,
I have to do my work first,
I'm going to be bored out of my wits,
When I go to secondary school,
You get it all the time,
Homework comes before everything else,
Even lunch!
Got to do my homework now,
Humph!

Heather Gibson (11) Whiteknights CP School

HOLIDAYS

At last! End of term,
No more school for a week,
at least,
Now on holiday I can relax,
And enjoy life.

Wake up late,
Sleep late,
Is what I will do,
I'll watch TV all day,
And have the best of fun.

Now I'm bored of telly,
I think I'll ride my bike,
Go down the shops,
And buy a few Pogs,
Or football stickers,
For only 23p.

The holiday's nearly over,
I've got to practise my piano,
and clarinet,
School tomorrow and,
Oh no!
Haven't done my homework!

Michael Mikhail (10) Whiteknights CP School

FIRST BORN

When I first came in the world
A cheer went round
My mum was exhausted
My dad was ecstatic
and I just wanted a drink
life was fine
everything around was mine
until a new baby came
and nothing was the same
as we got older another was born
What a shame
everything they did I got the blame
Gee!
Most of it wasn't me!
Life is such a pain.

Jessica Pritchard (11) Whiteknights CP School

MY BROTHER

My little brother is such a pain,
He calls me name after name,
He even has the darn right cheek,
To nick my pocket money every week,
He rants and raves like a bull gone mad,
It really really makes me very sad,
He tears my books and breaks my toys,
Oh why can't he be like other boys,
Even on my birthday he gets his own way,
Someday I tell him you'll have to pay,
If only he was sensible, calm and quiet,
Then maybe he wouldn't cause such a riot,
Well I suppose some days he is okay,
All right I exaggerated a bit of the *way!*

Christopher Longhorn (11) Whiteknights CP School

BUBBLES

Bubbles, bubbles, bubbles so colourful
so airy, so delicate and light, drifting
through the sky.

Colours of a rainbow reflected
from the light.

It flies across the sky. It's large
or small, round and it pops by the touch
of a finger.

Catherine Young (9) Wildridings Primary School

BUBBLES

Fantastic bubbles are in the air,
fantastic bubbles everywhere.
They are so colourful as the sun,
so pretty and delicate every one.
They have colours of rainbows,
breezes blow them high and low
they are shiny like the paddling pool.
What about their shiny light,
they will fly about till night!

Vikki Docherty (8) Wildridings Primary School

SPRING

Daffodils are yellow,
Bluebells are blue,
The sun is shining,
Lambs are due.

Blossoms are growing on the trees,
Branches are blowing with the breeze.

Hooray hooray it is spring again!

Hedgehogs are out of hibernation,
To come and join the celebration.

Buds are growing on the trees,
The flowers are growing with the leaves.

Hooray hooray it is spring again!

Birds are singing lovely notes,
The sound comes deeply from their throats.

Hooray hooray it is spring again!
Hooray hooray it is spring again!

Felicity Morris (9) Wildridings Primary School

BUBBLES

Big and round, small and
fat I drift carefully through
the sky, slippery, shiny, wet and
fragile. I pop when fingers
touch. I am like a tiny rainbow
and I'm very hard to catch
but I'll give you a second
chance.

Danielle Estcourt (9) Wildridings Primary School

IN MY BOX

In my box, I would keep.
My family because they are sweet.

In my box, I would keep.
Sunny days to keep me warm.

In my cupboard, I would keep.
Everlasting peace,
I would let it go when a war started.

In my cupboard, I would keep.
Friendships going.
Then I'll never be lonely.

In my box, I would keep.
All the sweets in the world
Then I'll never be hungry.

In my box, I would keep.
All the good days.
Because then I'll never forget them.

Alice Ludlow (10) Wildridings Primary School

THE FUTURE OF THE WORLD

Endangered animals will be free,
Bears, Tigers and things in the sea.
Different people will live together,
All in unity and forever.
There will be no more war,
Because of all the things I saw.
To this planet we'll do our best,
To make it better than the rest.

Christopher Hotson (9) Wildridings Primary School

DRACULA'S TOWER

In a dark and stormy hour,
A stranger goes to Dracula's tower.

A servant shows him to a room,
Full of cobwebs, spiders, dust and gloom.

But as the stranger goes to sleep,
The things around him begin to creep.

Skeletons with jangling chains,
Cold dead fingers and dead man's brains.

Shouting screaming all the night,
The poor old stranger dies of fright.

Now in the dark and stormy hours,
A new ghost haunts at Dracula's towers.

James Waring (9) Wildridings Primary School

SOUNDS OF THE WORLD

I'm scared of the owl hooting all night,
Under the glistening moon,
The howl of the big bad wolf,
Hiding behind the trees.
I'm scared of rustling noises of the leaves,
When the wind keeps whistling through them.

I love the noise of a beautiful harp being played all through the day.
I hate the noise of bombs and guns in the big big war.
I love the noise of the silent snow when it falls from the sky.
Oh what beautiful noises the world has,
I will listen forever more.

Laura Osman (9) Wildridings Primary School

WINTER IN THE PLAYGROUND

Winter in the playground
the ground is all white
it is all wet
and slushy too.

Everyone is running
and shouting
and at the end it snows
it is silent very silent
again.

Claire May (8) Wildridings Primary School

MY SNOWMAN

My snowman is
made out
of snow I watch
it melt silently.
It drips like water falling
from a tap.
But when the sun
comes out, my snowman is gone.

Carl Tingley (8) Wildridings Primary School

A BUBBLE'S VIEW

My life has its ups and downs,
Always downs when children are around.
They chase me, they pop me
They stamp on me
Apart from one girl
Called Chloe.
She is kind to me.
She holds me gently.

I'm glad when grown ups say how nice
That bubbles are
Because they glitter
In the golden sun.
I always know that I'm going to pop.
That's why I make the most of it,
And I speak for all the bubbles.

Robert Phelan (8) Wildridings Primary School

CATS ARE FUN

I know a little cat,
He's just such fun.
He jumps and runs and tumbles.
He's such a super cat!
He climbs, his fur shines.
Sometimes I think he's mine.
But he isn't. Sometimes I sit all day and
watch him
Even though he is not mine.
One day, perhaps, I'll get my wish,
And have a cat of my own.

Robert Escott (8) Wildridings Primary School

SPRING

Blossom is pink,
Tulips are blue,
Primroses are sweet,
Spring is good too.

Daffodils are yellow,
Snowdrops are white,
The sky is blue and spring is out,
Especially for you.

Sun is shining,
Lambs are born,
Flowers are out and,
The sun's shouting out,
      It's spring.

Birds will sing that,
Easter is near,
Hyacinths white and,
Celebration cheer.

Matthew East (9) Wildridings Primary School

WAR IN BURMA

My Grandpa fought in Burma, he was very brave.
He fought on and on for he had England to save.
There was lots of fighting and lots of blood.
Worse than a fire, worse than a flood.
He must have been relieved when the war had ended
Lots of wounded people had to be tended.
I hope it never starts again
And no more people have to be in pain.
But the main thing is, it's added to my pride.
He is my grandpa and he's alive!

Chloe Everall (8) Wildridings Primary School

A HOT AIR BALLOON

I opened my curtains and what did I see?
A hot air balloon looking at me.
From inside the basket I thought I could see
Somebody standing and waving at me.

The flickering flame started to roar
And then the balloon began to soar.
Higher and higher into the sky
'Oh look the balloon is beginning to fly!'

As the balloon flew up and away
The sparkling colours began to play
With the pinks and the blues now looking much lighter
Because the sun is shining much brighter.

The red and the greens were having such fun
With the twinkling light beams shot from the sun.
The hand from the basket began to flutter
The balloon went pop and fell into the gutter!

Claire Eastment (9) Woodley CE Primary School

SUMMER TIME

We can go canoeing in a
river and they might crash in
to you.
Sometimes you get sun burnt
when mum goes in she tips
the canoe up and we all get wet

Ian Gardener (8) Woodley CE Primary School

THE FUNERAL

. . . I couldn't believe it . . .
My Grandma had just died.
I went to her funeral . . .
It was all miserable and sad.
All around me people were crying,
It was a shock . . . for me anyway.
So many flowers by her dead body,
I felt trapped in between sadness and joy.
Why did she die . . . I ask myself.
Why o why did she die . . . I plead,
I deeply prayed that she could come back . . .
But I knew she couldn't.
My Grandad is all on his own,
I wish he wasn't.
A few weeks later I recovered,
But she will always be in my heart . . .

Carla Morley (11) Woodley CE Primary School

WHEN IT'S DARK

When it's dark
in the night,
and there's no
light, or anyone
in sight, and
a horrible monster
grabs you,
with pain and
in vain you
scream and scream,
but no-one comes.

Laura Home (8) Woodley CE Primary School

MY PARK

If I could have a park I know how it would be,
With birds and butterflies plus a big old tree.
The boys would play about,
The girls would laugh and shout.
A dog would gnaw a bone,
I'd sit upon a throne.
A pond with fishes,
I'd wash the dishes.
A church with a steeple,
I'd go with many people.
Slides and swings
And many other things
That is how my park would be.

Lindsay Clare Muscroft (9) Woodley CE Primary School

I SAW A SKELETON

I saw a skeleton.
How did I know I saw
him without any clothes.
He had some bones and
he was then so old
and then I never saw
him again.

Jillian Rankin (8) Woodley CE Primary School

COWBOY'S PREY

The cowboy saw the dusty road,
Along it hopped a massive toad,
This was the place he'd fight,
His enemy galloped into sight.

His hand sweated on the gun,
It was the opposite of fun,
He was frightened, he was scared,
He could not shoot for all he dared.

His enemy galloped past,
That moment seemed to last and last,
His enemy's bullet made of tin,
Just went underneath his chin.

He turned his horse right around
It made the most tremendous sound,
His enemy he shot straight after,
He could hear his enemy's laughter.

He was the one to gain,
Then he shot, his enemy writhed in pain
He shot again through his enemy's head
His enemy was surely dead.

Mark Saunders (10) Woodley CE Primary School

A CURTAIN

A curtain is a curtain
But it's black and white
A green shady curtain
Which I see in the night
It glows in the dark
Where is that curtain?
Is it black and white?
Or grey and white?
(I don't know?)

David Ian Riley (8) Woodley CE Primary School

HE'S MY BEST FRIEND

He's always there when I want him,
He's never away on holiday,
And he's my best friend.

He's always there in the evenings
And in the mornings too
He's there when I wake up,
And he's my best friend.

He's just so soft and cuddly,
That I take him to school,
And he's my best friend.

He comes camping when I do,
That's why he's always with me,
And he's my best friend.

He's always my friend and never away,
Just a pony for my best friend,
And he's my best friend.

Laura Viles (7) Woodley CE Primary School

HELP I'M LOST

I was lost in the woods,
Crying, alone.
I wanted someone to find me,
To take me home.
It was getting late, late at night,
I wished for somebody to come.
I heard a rustling in the bushes,
There stood mum.
I ran fast to her,
She disappeared.
It had happened, it was true,
Just as I'd feared.
She had a spell put on her,
By a wicked witch,
To break the spell was difficult.
I had to find a switch,
It was somewhere in the hall of mirrors.
Very hard to find,
But first I had to get out of the woods.
To get someone kind,
We fell about 100ft down,
And died.

Jenna Smith (10) Woodley CE Primary School

MY PENCIL CASE

In my pencil case there now must go,
rubbers, rulers, pencils and,
So I pack them all for school the next day.
Then I say that's ready for tomorrow,
and now I don't have to borrow.

Emily Aylward (9) Woodley CE Primary School

MY CAT

When my cat yawns
she stretches her claws she
meows out loud and
she reaches for the table
and scratches the
table and she pulls
the cloth down on
her head and
then she gets into
bed ZZZZZZZZZZZ
      meow.

Sarah Abraham (7) Woodley CE Primary School

THAT NIGHT

That night I was having fun,
That night I was dancing,
That night it was groovy,
That night I was laughing,
That night I had a pain in my head,
That night I nearly died,
That night it all happened,
That night it was scary,
That night I was in fear,
That night . . .
      That night . . .
           That night . . .
                  That night . . .
I could have died.

Charlie-Jane Bryant (10) Woodley CE Primary School

IN THE GARDEN

The flower grows in the garden
It gets food from the earth
When the sun shines it opens
Its petals they are pretty small and red
The birds fly in the sky
They dig in the garden for worms
They sing when they are happy.

Rebecca Bennett (8) Woodley CE Primary School

I'M LATE FOR WORK

My first day at work I'll get the sack,
My boss will break my lovely back.
There's people crowding all around me,
By the time I get there it'll be
Time for tea.
I can't hear enough to think,
I've hardly got time to even blink.
Get out of my way I'm on that train,
If only my work was down a
Quiet country lane.
Phew I've made it at last,
Come on driver I need to get to
London fast.
Now I'm finally at work,
They will all think that I am a berk.

Sam Cialis (11) Woodley CE Primary School

ALONE

Being alone in a deserted town.
The moon light man has left for now.
The cold night air stings your cheeks.
The cold is in your bones it makes you weak.
You look around but no-one's there.
Evil shadows stop and stare.
Empty alleys await danger.
Longing for a midnight stranger.
You're all on your own with nowhere to go.
The midnight town which only ghosts own.
You're all alone.
You hear a sound and look around.
Hearts beat faster, this is a midnight disaster.
The wind is getting stronger.
You want to get out.
You hear a scream, you give a shout.
Let me out.
Oh no the spell is broken the ghosts are now out,
Shouts and screams go all around.
Shadows appear on the walls thin and tall.
And they're coming for me.
I'm all alone with nowhere to go.
I try to run but the damage is done.
I'm all alone with nowhere to run.
For I am alone!

Michelle Bennett (11) Woodley CE Primary School

RUSHING PEOPLE

There are people rushing around
People lost and people found
Late for interviews or trains
And it doesn't help when it rains.
Playing music in the town
Everyone coming to gather round
Everyone who gathers round
Listens to the lovely sound.
People don't care about others
Even people run without mothers.

Anthony Thompson (10) Woodley CE Primary School

IN THE NIGHT

In the night I had a fright
I screamed and shut my eyes tight
I turned on my light.
It was that rain again
What a pain
It is always that rain
Tapping on my window pane.

Laura Tysoe (9) Woodley CE Primary School

IF ONLY

If the moon was a door knob
I would go into the dark misty passage in the door.

If the moon was a bridge I would
cross over to another world.

If the clouds were sheep
I would make a sweater out of their wool.

If the sea was lemonade I would
share it with the homeless, Sarah and Rebecca.

Katherine Williams (8) Woodley CE Primary School

BUSY PEOPLE

People rushing all around
dashing darting round and round
more and more people come
running racing up and down
people coming racing running
dashing darting racing running
sliding skidding what a rush
suddenly they all dash off.

Becky Viles (10) Woodley CE Primary School

MY PET CAT

My pet cat
Has a big black hat
When he's tired he sits on a mat
When he's bored he chases a rat
Then he goes and kills a bat
My pet cat is big and fat.

Rosanne Warner (9) Woodley CE Primary School

THE TEDDY BEAR POEM

Teddy bear, teddy bear turn around
Teddy bear, teddy bear touch the ground
Teddy bear, teddy bear say good night
Teddy bear, teddy bear go to sleep
Teddy bear, teddy bear breakfast time
Teddy bear, teddy bear let's go out
Teddy bear, teddy bear let's go to the pond and
We saw a fish and the fish went

Splash

Teddy bear, teddy bear say goodbye.

Kelly Warwick (8) Woodley CE Primary School

LOSING

We lost the war a pity I know
I did it for my country though
The deserted battleland
is plain and dry
our captain is dead
I wonder if we'll get free
maybe a miracle will save
us maybe a miracle won't
but as long as I know
I did it for my country
Most of my friends are dead
They have been shot or stabbed
If you read this rescue me.

Scott Weal (10) Woodley CE Primary School

LATE FOR WORK

People dancing round and round
Rushing, hurrying along the ground
It's my first day at work
Will I make it, yes I will
Come on train, go faster
If I'm late I'll get the sack.

Yes I've made it, got to catch the
Bus now, oh no it's late
Must run, I've got to make it
Phew! I'm there at last
I must have a sit down.

Stephen Parker (10) Woodley CE Primary School

LOOKING FOR THE STONE

Open the door round the corner.
Still I think I'm getting warmer.
Is it this door or is it that?
Oh crumbs watch out low flying bat.
It's over here come on quick.
Come on run don't trip on the stick.
Come on it's just up those stairs.
Crikey! We're surrounded by bears.
Let's just grab the stone
Or we'll just end up as bone.
Ok I've got it jump down here.

Richard Tollman (11) Woodley CE Primary School

THE SUMMER

The birds cheep
And make the morning radiant
And bright,
When the birds fly the sun shines.
When the sun shines
the trees grow in delight
and the leaves flow in the air.

Thomas Goodey (8) Woodley CE Primary School

MY NAN

Nan, my Nan,
Can sit and knit and knit
and knit.
Look at it.
Who will it fit?
'Crocodiles?' Nan smiles.
'Snakes?' Nan shakes.
'Gorillas going out?'
Nan falls about.
Who's it for, Nan?
Who?
'It's for you love.
You.
'Oo!'

Charlotte Evans (9) Woodley CE Primary School

THE SEAWEED POEM

When we go to the seaside we will have lots
of fun eating our lunch.
Playing around in the sea popping
Seaweed collecting shells, making sandcastles
But one of the best things is playing in the big waves,
jumping over them but then
I'm too tired for anything.

George Hood (8) Yattendon School

THE SEA

The sea is like an underground world,
Sparkling stones,
And noises I have never heard.
Flying fish,
They look so strange.
I wish I lived in the sea,
The water sparkles,
Sometimes it's as smooth as leather
Sometimes it's as rough as a brick.

Thomas Wills (8) Yattendon School

IN THE PLAYGROUND

In the playground,
I'm all alone.
No-one to play with or talk to.
So I just walk.
I walk on stilts maybe,
Or skip with a rope,
Perhaps bounce a ball,
Then I sit on the wall,
Hoping not to fall.
I play on the bars
Watching the cars.
I climb up trees
Staining my knees.
Then the bell rings,
And I try to swing
off the trees
Pulling off leaves - poor things!

Faye Bethan Smith (9) Yattendon School

IN THE PLAYGROUND

Out in the playground I have nothing to do,
Except wandering around and looking about.
Or maybe I will bounce a netball
or go and sit on the wall.
I wonder how many people will ask me to play?
Or maybe nobody will pass this way.
I could watch the cars
or draw some stars
Until my friend comes out to play.

Lesley King (11) Yattendon School

THE SEA SHELL

I
was
hit. I was
damaged by the
rocks, as my shiny
surface wore away.
I saw a dolphin, then
a fish, a rainbow trout,
and followed by a crab.
All this time, I was
under the sea, waiting
to land on the
beach.

Laura Collett (9) Yattendon School

IN THE PLAYGROUND

In the playground.
Children play.
Some with stilts.
Some prance away.
Infants run
All for fun.
But some choose to walk
And some like to talk.
Juniors are fit,
Others just sit,
On the wall.
'Careful not to fall!'
Children trip over
Like a leaf turning.
Children on the bars
Are like monkeys.
In the shining, shivering sand.
Children jump and there they land.
Then the bell rings
And the children
Rush into line,
Like a noisy gale of wind.

Lindsay Wakefield (10) Yattendon School

THE NEST

Don't move
Don't speak
Look at that beak.
As yellow as gold,
Waiting to be fed,
Then look it's in bed.
As snug as a bug.

Hannah Keogh (8) Yattendon School

DARK

The dark creeps slowly.
Like a panther stalking its prey,
As quiet as a mouse,
But as deadly as a knife.
Then when he's unaware,
Darkness strikes one fatal blow,
And the golden crusader retreats.
Darkness has won, or has he?

James Ash (11) Yattendon School

AT PLAY TIME

I lean against the wall.
I'm bored
I see the others playing ball.
I ask if I can play
But they say 'Go away!'
I go and see if I can play
With someone else.
But there's no-one.
I hear the bell ring
So I go in.

George Wood (8) Yattendon School

INFORMATION

We hope you have enjoyed reading this book - and that you will continue to enjoy it in the coming years.

If you like reading and writing poetry drop us a line, or give us a call, and we'll send you a free information pack.

    Poetry Now (Young Writers) Information
              1-2 Wainman Road
                  Woodston
                Peterborough
                    PE2 7BU